CRISPY WINTERS
&
UNBROKEN SHELLS

by Amanda Kroll

PublishAmerica
Baltimore

First printing

At the specific preference of the author, PublishAmerica allowed this work to remain exactly as the author intended, verbatim, without editorial input.

ISBN: 1-4241-9861-5
PUBLISHED BY PUBLISHAMERICA, LLLP
www.publishamerica.com
Baltimore

Printed in the United States of America

Introduction

Crispy Winters & Unbroken Shells is my episodic journey from toddler to college graduate. These episodes are entries recorded from my perspective during that time in my life and mature as I grow older.

Reliving these experiences has been both therapeutic and enlightening. Memories from age three are stronger and have more feeling than any memory I have had since then. Perhaps it is the little things that children notice that adults take for granted that make these memories so strong.

Recording these experiences has helped me gain a clearer understanding of who I am and what my future should be. It has helped me accept some of my limitations due to epilepsy by focusing on the strengths of my character.

I want to thank my sister, Angela, for always being my best friend, and my mom for making my strongest memories the best ones.

Contents

Chapter 1

Leaves and Snoopy

Outside the little white house...

The grass is a little wet, and really green. The sidewalk goes on forever. Bugs are everywhere. There are lots of little sticks that have lines where they break apart. With my toddler fingers I grab the twig and snap it easily where it comes apart. The roly-poly on the cracked sidewalk crawls away from me. I put the twig in front of him. He climbs on for a ride. I bring him to me. He curls into a ball. The lines on his curved body disappear. Suddenly I am picked up and carried inside.

The Swamp...

Mommy tells us that Uncle Chucky's boat is called a canoe. I get my own seat and a place on the bottom of the canoe to put my feet, but my legs are too short so my feet are hanging. I'm wearing a squishy orange thing called a life server because I'm too little to know how to swim. Sissy's wearing one, too. So is Uncle Chucky. Mommy didn't get one because there weren't enough. I scoot to one side of the boat and tightly hold onto the edge so I won't fall off my seat. Uncle

Chucky pushes the canoe into the swamp water and then hops inside it. He grabs a paddle and sweeps the water with it. I peek over the edge. The water is goopy and green. I look up. All around me there are droopy plants that hang down and into the swamp.

I'm bored. The slow rocking of Uncle Chucky's canoe makes me sleepy. I slide down onto the floor, safely tucked between the seats. I look up. All I can see is the sky and Sissy sitting in my seat.

I wake up. Mommy's yelling at Uncle Chucky. We're not in the canoe anymore. Mommy tells everyone that a giant alligator—as big as two canoes—almost ate us. Sissy tells me that the alligator moved slowly next to the canoe and then went under it. Everyone tried to be as quiet as possible, but then Uncle Chucky thought it would be funny to rock the boat a little. The alligator ignored us and then floated away, but Mommy's still mad. And I missed all of it!

Jacksonville…

I live in a place called Jacksonville, North Carolina. Mommy says our small house is faded and peeling from old age, but it looks perfect to me. Sissy and I were born here three years ago. She's my twin sister and my best friend. Our first word was Sissy. Then it was Mammamama…. Then it was giraffe and elephant because of the animal poster that Mommy put on our wall above our playpen. Then we ate it. It looked a lot like candy. Mommy lived in Jacksonville when she was little, too. She lived in one of the upstairs bedrooms in Grandma and Grandpop's big yellow house, five houses down from us. It has a huge tree stump in the yard that fits both Sissy and me. We're almost too big for it now. Sometimes we go to the park. There are so many trees making so much shade that it looks like nighttime all the time. My favorite adventure is when Mommy takes us to the beach. The trees disappear and everywhere there are weeds. There's more of a breeze and it has a salty smell.

Tea sets...

They are the cutest little tea sets we have—not glass or china like Grandma has—they are tiny orange and yellow and red Tupperware cups with little plates that go underneath the bowls. Mommy gives us crackers to eat with our water that we pretend is tea. We dress up, too, in the princess dresses that Grandma made us. They have crisscross squares on them and poof out at the bottom like Cinderella dresses.

At Mrs. Mary's...

Our babysitter, Mrs. Mary, is cooking them again. Leaves. Who eats leaves? What if there are bugs on them? Sissy looks worried, too. We eat them and go play outside. Her boy is watching us.

One of us asks him why he's so dark. "You see this?" He picks up a handful of dirt. "I eat this every day." He turns to the side and it looks like he tosses it into his mouth.

We look hesitantly at the dirt, then look at each other and decide to accept his unspoken challenge. We take a handful and touch it with our tongues. We spit it out.

The boy laughs and we feel foolish, but we still believe him.

Mommy picks us up and we keep the dirt story to ourselves. But we do tell her that Mrs. Mary is making us eat leaves. Surprised and confused, Mommy says nothing until she takes us to Mrs. Mary's house again and sees her at the sink, washing dark green leafy collards. Mommy tries to keep from laughing as Sissy and I whisper, "Look there, Mommy! See? Leaves!"

Coloring contest...

It's *my* turn to win! I'm careful to color side to side and not up and down, side-to-side, and then midways because only little kids and people who can't do art do that. Sissy will beat me because everyone thinks she's the best artist. She's good. But I want to win this time! I remember not to color too hard because artists color light, like they don't want the crayon to touch the paper. I mess up. On the grass. Coloring grass is hard because it goes up and down, but I already colored everything side to side. Now I *know* Sissy's going to win. Maybe I can beat her if I use the best colors. I color the horse a pretty purple.

Sissy won. She won $50 for when she turns thirteen. I got second place. I got a ribbon.

The day before Easter...

There it stands, high on the ground like a candy firecracker. The rich smell draws me in and the only thing keeping me from ripping into the basket right now is Mommy in the room. So I wait. And wait. When she finally leaves the room, I grab the basket and tear off the plastic on the giant chocolate bunny first. I chomp on its head, body, tail and feet. My stomach rumbles. I rip open the plastic on the sugary marshmallow bunnies, and minutes later I've swallowed the peanut butter chocolate eggs, caramel rabbits and chocolate eggs and bunnies. I pull out the paper, ribbons, boxes and tin foil. Nothing. My stomach rumbles. Content, I fall asleep on the living room rug. I wake up the next morning to Sissy's squeals of delight. "I gotta Easter basket!"

I can't move. My stomach is turning this way and that. As I lay unmoving in my bed, I tell myself I will never again eat so much candy so fast.

Daycare (naps and crafts)...

When Mommy first dropped us off at daycare, we didn't know what to do. Sissy and I stuck together. But now we always run to the chest in the corner with all the clothes in it. Sissy puts on her favorite artsy smock and I put on my oversized green army shirt that's rough to the touch, like a tent. They're really old, but fun to play with.

Sometimes after our nap we get to do crafts. I'm making a picture frame out of popsicle sticks and seashells. In it is a picture of me and Sissy in our costumes. Sissy's wearing a green hat—a jungle hat.

Jamie…

Jamie is my best friend. She has straight hair like me, only it's dark brown and shorter than mine. It looks like a bowl on her head. She smells like a baby, but she's really nice. She shares her food and her thermos with me. Her mommy makes her yummy lunches with cookies and cupcakes and chips. Mommy only makes me healthy food, with no cookies or candy. Jamie's thermos has Kool-Aid, not boring milk like mine. She even shared it with me when she was sick. Mommy told me not to drink out of the same cup as a sick person, so I drank from the opposite side that she drank from. I still got sick and Mommy guessed why.

Jamie's mommy is loud. She hates me and makes fun of me because I blink too much. Once when I was visiting Jamie, I was standing in her driveway and her mommy ordered me to stop blinking. She said I looked silly. I almost cried because I couldn't stop. I felt like I was spacing out and I was feeling dizzy and I couldn't hear what she was saying. But I could still see her mimicking me. I hate her. I hope she never tells Mommy that I didn't listen to her.

On the N.C. coast…

I can always smell the ocean before I get there and see the weeds that spring up, telling me we're getting closer. They tell Sissy, too, and we both get excited and squeal, "We're here! We're here!"

The warm soft sand tickles my feet and squeezes between my toes. I love to stand where the water comes in over my feet, then backs away. Little sucky things crawl under my feet and I jump away because it feels funny. Mommy walks with us and buys an ice cream cone for all of us to share. It's fun. My white-blonde hair is in a ponytail so it doesn't fly into my ice cream, but sometimes a hair comes undone and sticks to my face. Sometimes it's cold out here, but most of the time at least the sand feels a little warm. Sissy and I look brown from the sun. We look for shark's teeth, tiny and black. A wet black that shines in my hand. I wonder how tiny the sharks are to fit into these teeth. We look for unbroken shells and go up to the dock and see how far the ocean goes before hitting the sky. I see boats at the end of the ocean. It doesn't look too far. The water is darker out there and smoother. The water is too deep under the dock to play in, and Mommy says there's probably broken glass under there, anyway, and that it's nicer just to sit and watch the ocean.

Down the street...

"Come on, girls. We're going to Grandma's house."

"Yay! Do you think Grandma will take out her teeth again?" I love it when Grandma tries to scare us that way. It always works. Why does she want to wear pretend teeth?

We ride uphill on our bright red tricycles. We go halfway up the street before getting off and walking the rest of the way. It's only a few houses away—I can almost see the stump in her yard from our little house with the cracked sidewalk. Whenever I'm at Grandma's house, I stay inside, except when we jump in the piles of raked leaves in the fall. Sometimes I follow Grandma into the garage where she keeps the blueberries she grows in the backyard garden. She tells me stories about swamp alligators just past the backyard. Sissy and I stay away from there. Grandma shows me how to stay quiet in front of the screen door so the squirrels won't be afraid to come up and let us feed them. The big reason why I stay inside is because of all the mosquitoes that leave tons of bites all over me, even on the parts of my arms that are covered.

My favorite time to visit Grandma is Christmas. We stay there a few days and sleep in the bedrooms on the second floor in Uncle Mikey's old room. It's filled with model ships that make me dream of faraway places and pirates. The bathroom's full of powder and pink fuzzy and fluffy stuff, like the toilet seat cover, carpet, shower curtain and other little flowery things.

Downstairs the families squeeze into the living room, talking about "the children" like we can't hear them. Wheel of Fortune is on TV and all the other kids are bored. We eat dinner in the dining room. Grandma and Grandpop only use it for holidays, so we're not allowed to be in there on other days. I help set out the expensive silverware and plates. There are other glasses and plates and bowls in the glass cabinets, but they're never used, just to look at. I don't like this room very much. Every time I go in here to explore, I'm yelled at. The Christmas tree is in the living room corner, next to the TV. It reaches the ceiling and hides all kinds of colorfully wrapped presents. Some of the grown-ups say that they're from Santa. I don't believe in Santa, but Grandma and Grandpop seem to, so I play along with them. Sissy and I always have matching presents; only with clothes I get yellow or blue and Sissy gets purple and pink. Those are our favorite colors.

The next morning Grandma either gives us cereal or makes us dippy eggs. We eat at the kitchen table in a tiny section of the kitchen. Sometimes we peel off bits of the old wallpaper when we're bored. Since we get bored a lot, Grandpop lets us play with the little green army men in their fold-up camp that he keeps in the closet from when our uncles were little.

Sissy and I do a lot of things to keep busy. We get a chalkboard and make a spiral and pretend that we're going through time. I'm Superman (because I think it would be fun to fly) and Sissy's Wonder Woman. Other times we play tea party.

When Mommy goes to work, Sissy and I swim in the swimming pool that Grandma has. We have to be careful not to lean on the sides, or else the water will leak out. Or we'll fall over into the grass.

Grandma and Grandpop's bookstore...

Sissy and I are at Grandma and Grandpop's bookstore. It's called, "Johnson's Christian Family Bookstore." It's lots of fun, even though we get bored a lot. I always hide underneath the loft in the children's section, where no grownups can reach me. It's nice to sleep there or daydream. My next favorite thing to do there is watch the cartoon, The Lion, the Witch, and the Wardrobe.

We're playing around toward the front of the store when I see Superman walk in. Not in his red and blue outfit, just in regular clothes. I grab Sissy's arm and yank her behind a row of bookmarks. I point at the man and whisper loudly, "Look! It's Superman!"

Sissy looks where I'm pointing. "No, it's not."

"Yes, it is! He's got the curl and everything!"

"Where's his cape?"

"He's in disguise, remember?"

We follow him around the bookstore, darting behind bookshelves whenever he looks our way. Superman stops at the register, which means he's about to leave. This will be my only chance. I muster up all my courage and walk up to the counter. I look up at him. "Mister?" He looks down at me and smiles. If I ask him if he's Superman, he'll say no to protect his disguise. "What's your name?" I finally ask him.

"Clark Kent," he replies and gives me an even bigger smile. I catch my breath and look back at Sissy, whose mouth is open in surprise. I give her an 'I told you so' look. I smile at Superman and run back to Sissy.

Mommy marries Superman...

Sissy, Mommy and I are all changing our last name from Gurley to Mellott, after my new daddy. We're standing in nice clothes in an empty room. The man who's with Mommy and Daddy asks us if we want to change our name. I think he's supposed to ask us, like he's asking for our permission or something. We're only four, so Sissy and I just nod our heads and smile shyly.

Now we do things like going camping and hiking. Once, Daddy even killed a snake! It was so cool! Mommy got sick.

Camping on the beach is my favorite. We eat bologna sandwiches on the picnic table we found there. Daddy sets up the tents. There are two. Mommy and Daddy are in one and Sissy and I are in the other. It's too cold to go in the water, so I put on my lemon yellow flip flops and walk to where the water comes onto the shore. I jump out of the way. Before we go to sleep, Daddy tells us about tidal waves. I think the ocean is wonderful! I fall asleep to the sound of crashing waves.

A new house...

Our new daddy is a marine and we're moving to a marine base in Chapel Hill, away from Grandma and Grandpop. They tell us that we'll still be able to visit them.

Our new house is a lot bigger than our old one. It has an upstairs, like in Grandma and Grandpop's house! The living room is huge and there are pretty stairs leading to the bedroom that Sissy and I share. Across from our room is Mommy and Daddy's bedroom. We have a bathroom both upstairs and downstairs. The one downstairs doesn't have a bathtub, though. Sissy and I have bunkbeds. I took the top one. I like that best because I feel like no one can reach me there. But Sissy's is neat, too. We can turn it into a fort by hanging blankets off my bed. I love doing that! Plus, she doesn't have to climb to the top like I do. But I like climbing, so it's not too bad.

There is no yard at our new house. We can't play anywhere because the houses are too close together. The bushes in front of the house have honeysuckle flowers on them. I take the flower part, turn it over to where the stem is sticking out, and suck the honey out. It's sweet and thin, not strong and thick like real honey. It's safe, too, not like poisonous berries. Sissy and I try to find all the honeysuckles and suck the honey out of them.

Barbie…

I'm sitting in the tub and taking a bath. Actually, I'm playing, but I told Mommy that I'm still washing. I'm playing with my Barbie doll. She has really long legs. She reminds me of the twigs I used to break when we lived at the old house. I dunk Barbie under the water to see if her hair gets wet like mine. It's stringy and rough now, definitely not like mine. I wonder what she'd look like if I cut her hair, but I don't want Mommy mad at me, so I won't do it. Besides, if I cut her hair off, how would I put it back? Mommy walks back into the bathroom and catches me drowning Barbie. She takes the doll away from me and I slowly start washing myself.

I never got my doll back. Mommy says she doesn't think I should have a Barbie doll, but she doesn't tell me why. I complain that Sissy gets to keep her Skipper doll, but she says that it's different. I guess Mommy's mad at me for drowning Barbie.

First grade…

First grade is scary. There are lots of loud kids and we have to learn so many rules I'm afraid I'll forget. This is different than daycare or kindergarten. Instead of letting us play, the teacher makes us sit in hard desks and talks to us every day. She's always asking us questions and making us learn to spell our names, like we don't already know how. I like her, though. She's nice to me. Her name is

Mrs. Gregory and she has big hair and a big nose with holes the size of pennies. I don't like that the teachers put Sissy in a different room. I keep to myself and wait until I see her again. One day I saw her and yelled, "Hey, Sissy!" She got mad and told me never to call her that anymore. That hurt my feelings. She told me that she was embarrassed and wants me to call her Angela, but that feels too weird, so I'm going to call her just "Sis." She's always been Sissy to me. In fact, that was our first word. Calling her Sis is hard, but I guess I'll get used to it.

Snoopy...

My lunchbox isn't Strawberry Shortcake or Barbie or even Carebears. I got Charlie Brown kicking a football past Snoopy on his doghouse. It's metal and always smells of peanut butter and jelly sandwiches and bananas. The other kids get cupcakes and cookies with their lunch, but I only get fruit. I wish Mommy would give me cookies or chocolate treats like the other kids get.

That's how lunch is. Everyone takes out their yummy lunches, trades, then chows down. I open my lunchbox. I see an apple next to my sandwich. Yesterday it was a banana. I don't think anybody will want to trade their cupcake for my apple. I take out my sandwich and eat it first. I like it when Mommy makes peanut butter and *butter* and jelly. I love butter! Mommy said that when I was little, I grabbed a stick of butter from a butter dish and actually ate the whole thing without getting sick. I pick up my apple. I love the juice and the way it crunches! I decide to eat the whole thing, even though I know I'll feel sick later. My stomach gets tight and the apple taste in my throat makes me sick. Next time I'll eat only a few bites.

My new brother...

Mommy's huge now. Sis and I are going to have a new baby brother. Mommy and Daddy want to name him Ram. They think it will be a cool name. That's what Daddy's marine friends call him because his initials on his duffel bag are R.A.M. Mommy says something about it being in the Bible, but I don't remember anything in there about a Ram. It's probably in the boring chapters, where there are a bunch of names and nothing else.

I have a dream that I'm in the neighbor's house. Even though I walk in the front door, I'm still sneaking in. I go upstairs and see socks everywhere. When I go downstairs, I see them boiling something in a big pot on the stove. I'm on the stairs and I can see something in there. I concentrate and realize it's a person. A baby. Somehow I know that it's my unborn baby brother. My heart's racing and I run out of the house. I feel sick. I find myself away from the house, outside, looking at it from across the street. Mommy and Sis are walking toward the house. I want to warn them not to go there because the neighbors are dangerous, but I can't speak. Then I wake up about to cry, but as always, I don't. I don't tell Mommy about the dream. It would scare her. I keep it to myself. Some time later Mommy says that the neighbors have something in the air in their yard that's dangerous to be around for too long, especially for her. She tells us to stay away from there.

Not long after that, Daddy drives Mommy to the hospital. We go with her, and her friend Kim watches us. We actually get to watch Ram being born. But when Mommy starts to yell, we get scared and Kim takes us outside the room and we wait in the hall with her. Soon Ram is born. Everything is different after that. He looks like a doll, except he's real. He's wrinkly and frowns all the time. His face was purple when he was born and his hair was black. After a few weeks go by, he gets bigger and doesn't frown as much, but he doesn't smile much, either. His hair is blond now, but his face is still purple when he cries. He screams too much and he's stinky. Mommy uses cloth diapers and is teaching me and Sis how to change the baby even though we're only seven.

We're in Pennsylvania now, visiting Daddy's family. They're really weird. Except for Melody, his sister. She's fun. It's snowing here. Sunday we go to their church. On our way to the car from the church, Melody takes my hand and we slide across the ice. It's so much fun. Our jeans get dirty and I have nothing else with me to wear. So now I'm stuck wearing my cousin's pants. It doesn't matter that he's a boy. We're the same size and that's all they care about. It's very woodsy here and the house is small. It wouldn't feel so small if there weren't so many people here. I'm scared of his mom. She's much bigger than me and likes to tell people what to do. She doesn't think Mommy should breastfeed Ram, even though Mommy told me that's what mommies are supposed to do. I wonder, how else are babies supposed to eat?

Tennessee...

Daddy got transferred and we moved to another state. Our house is a lot smaller than the one on the last marine base. Mommy listens to slow music all the time when she cleans the house.

I don't like it here. There's nothing to do. It's summertime, and another boring day tricks me into thinking that going on a bike ride to the store with Daddy will make it less boring. I like the rides there and back, but it's boring in between.

I climb on the back and he takes off. I hold on tight, but he doesn't notice that I'm about to fall off. I try to enjoy the ride, but where do I put my feet? What if they get caught in the wheel? I'll go flying and end up with no feet!

Finally we're at the grocery store. Daddy sets his bike aside and goes inside. I want another ride!

Another school...

Our new school is almost like my old school. It looks different, but we do a lot of the same things. I don't make any friends because I'm too shy. To make things worse, Sis and I are in a speech class with a bunch of other kids that don't know how to talk right. We can't say our 'Rs'. Mommy says that we sound like we're from Boston. I don't know where that is, but this girl in the class who can't say her 'S's keeps teasing us.

Except for Speech class, Sis and I are in separate classrooms again. She has a nice teacher named Mrs. Shepherd. She's teaching Sis and her classmates all of the Lord's Prayer. I'm glad I don't have to learn it. I hate memorizing stuff. We do fun stuff in my class. On Valentine's Day, we passed around Valentine's Day cards and candy to all the kids in the class.

I learn how to add by imagining dice and count the dots as quickly as I can in my head. Everyone else just memorizes the numbers, but this way I don't have to. The teacher doesn't know that I do it differently because I'm so fast. So fast, in fact, that I win the daily math contest. I feel so much pressure to be as quick as possible, though, because that's how a person wins. I don't like it. I could keep winning, but I'm tired of going so fast. The losers get to sit out and watch. They don't have to do anything. So I slow down and let someone else win. I feel so much calmer now.

I look outside the window a lot. I wonder what's out there. The field outside, past the playground where the kids play, is all grass. During recess, I go there and pick flowers. I tie them together into knots and make a flower necklace. I do this every day. I never play on the playground. I like being by myself. When our class goes on a field trip, I'm always last in line. I never have to lead because I'm the shortest.

The teacher tells us that we're going to be in an assembly. I'm nervous at first, but now I'm having fun making my costume. I'm an

Indian and I get to wear a brown costume and carry a papoose. After we do a skit with our costumes and canoes, we change out of our costumes. Then we sing, Miss Molly Malone and other songs that don't make any sense to me. This is so much fun!

Glasses...

I'm nervous. I don't want to go into my classroom. Where else can I go? I push my new glasses up on my nose. They feel clunky, but Mommy says I'll get used to them. I picked out a brown pair with a picture of Lucy from Charlie Brown on the side. I walk into the classroom. I keep my head down, hoping nobody will notice.

"Oh, how cute!" I look up and see this big girl smiling at me. "You look so adorable with those glasses!" The other kids agree. I relax and sit in my desk. I smile. *Wearing glasses isn't so bad after all.*

Roaches and ants...

We're moving to sunny California! I'm glad we're moving again. I don't want to stay in this house. It had roaches, then ants, and now has roaches again. I hate bugs. They're ugly and get into everything. Living here wasn't all bad, though. Once the whole marine base flooded and people swam in the streets for fun. They were in their swimsuits and everything. I wanted to go outside, too, but Mommy wouldn't let me. I never get to do anything!

Chapter 2

El Toro Marine Brats

Playing with Ram...

Ram is old enough now that we can push him around in his diaper box. He loves it! Sis and I are nine and Ram's two. He's so big now, I can't hold him anymore! The only time I don't like being around him is when mom runs errands and takes us with her. When we went to the commissary, he was throwing a temper tantrum and screaming for his raisins. He likes the ones that come in those little red boxes. We have tons of those at home for him to snack on. We don't have sweets. Even at church Ram gets into trouble. Once Mom looked next to her and he had disappeared. He had slid underneath the pews all the way to the pulpit. Mom tapped a wooden spoon against the pew. We heard Ram's little voice from up front. "Ooh, she means it this time!"

Mom got him a boy cabbage patch doll named Samuel. He calls it his 'little brother.' I guess he got tired of being the littlest one in the house and having only sisters. Dad doesn't like the fact that Ram has a doll that he takes it with him wherever he goes. Ram wants to take his new little brother everywhere!

At Woodbridge Community Church...

Every single oldie seems to be singing for me since I met Jonathan. I especially like the song, Johnny Angel. He has a wonderful smile, chocolate brown eyes, and a helicopter laugh. And he's so tall! I'm in love. I met him in Sunday school. Jonathan is the oldest of three boys in a perfect family. They look like they have a lot more money than we do. The boys even wear suits to church. His dad seems nice. And tall. Very, very tall. His mom's friendly and tall, too. She works at the hospital that Mom took me to. I felt embarrassed to have his mom see me sick. I hope she won't tell him. I was diagnosed with acute scoliosis. I panicked and now I sit and stand up straight all the time.

All the girls like Jonathan. Even Sis. He still acts annoying like any other boy, running around and crashing into people. But when he crashed into me, he stopped, turned to me and asked if I was okay because I was holding hot chocolate. I smiled. Of course I was okay! *He* was talking to me. He smiled back, then ran to join his obnoxious friends who yelled at him for talking to a girl.

The girl from Japan...

I'm kinda glad we're trading Dad for Takako. Dad's gone to Okinawa and it's quieter. Takako's a foreign exchange student from Tokyo, Japan.

I wait by the door, dressed up like I'm going to church. Takako walks in, followed by Mom. Takako's shy and smart with tan skin and short black hair. I like her right away. She hands us lots of presents! She says it's the custom in her country to give gifts. I think I'll visit Japan someday. She gives us kimonos, candy, and a Japanese toy that's too hard to play. She gives us rice candy, too. I try to take off the wrapper, but my hands get all sticky. She laughs and tells me that I'm supposed to eat the wrapper. I try another piece. It tastes funny. I show her everything—my xylophone and my brother,

Ram. He can't say her name because he's too little. When he tries to say her name, it comes out as "Tako," which means octopus in Japanese. I show her my toys, then Mom and Dad's waterbed. She's never seen one before. I tell her to sit down. She sits and the mattress starts to sink. She jumps up and stares at the bed like it's going to eat her.

Takako shows us a picture of her boyfriend. She's too shy to say much about him, though.

Takako's been really busy going to a university and talking with other Japanese girls at the exchange program. I don't get to hang out with her at all. I wish I were older, so she would hang out with me, too.

Buddha...

I'm so excited! Takako's coming to church with us and I want to show her everything—my Sunday school room, the piano in the basement that I can play church songs on, the big room where we have potlucks every night, the church part with the pews and organs and hymnals, and the stained glass windows with pictures of Jesus holding kids and baby sheep.

Takako is smiling now. I don't fall asleep in church. Ever. But it's boring right now. The pastor keeps saying "Jesus is God," like I forgot since last week. I squirm. I want to show Takako everything. *Hurry up*! I want her to like everybody here, and for everybody to be nice to her.

It's finally over. Everyone says hi to Takako and ignores me. I want to play songs for Takako on the piano downstairs, but this lady won't stop talking to her.

I'm mad on the way home. I didn't get to show Takako anything! Mom ignores me and asks her what she thought of church. She's frowning, but I don't know why. Probably because we left too soon and she didn't get to spend any time with me. She's quiet, then says, "Buddha is God." I don't know who Buddha is, but I don't say anything because Mom has that "grownups only" look on her face.

Allergies...

Mom makes her own avocado dip before Takako leaves. Everyone seems to like it but me. Mom makes me finish it even though I don't want to. It tastes okay, I just don't feel good. I run to the bathroom and throw up. I can't believe I got sick right in front of Takako. I feel so embarrassed. She feels sorry for me and gives me her pretty handkerchief with flowers on it. I feel stupid.

Takako went home and I'm really sad. Dad's back. It feels weird seeing him again, like I don't know him. He gives us kimonos that are too big.

A bedtime story...

I wait. And wait. And wait. But it just keeps getting worse for the poor family. When Dad finishes reading the last page, I sit up in disbelief.

"That was the worst story I ever heard!"

"Why? Because it didn't have a happy ending? Steinbeck points out the sad reality that greed corrupts people and blinds others until it's too late. Think about it." He tucks me in and leaves me to my thoughts. *Why did the writer mess up those people's lives like that? Why did he make that family think that they're gonna be rich and finally happy, and then decide to kill everybody in the story? Greed? I don't understand. It was an accident! I feel really sad now. I want a happy ending!*

I fall asleep dreaming of different endings, where I save the people from their misery and help them start a better life.

At the after-school care...

I think it's pretty cool that my new friend's name is Steven King, but he doesn't make a big deal out of it. He's my match at handball. It's a good game, like racquetball, only the ball's the size of a soccer ball and it's red and really bouncy. And we use our hands. The fist, actually, is the best way. The moves are kind of like volleyball, only we aim at a wall—the same one we use for dodge ball—and it takes a lot of readiness, quick legs, and tough knuckles. Yeah, the afterschool care is *definitely* more fun—a lot more fun than I thought it would be. I wish Jonathan could see how fast I am at this game. And dodge ball, too. But I get tense during the whole game since I'm not sure where the ball's going to go. It's like a firing squad! I'm usually one of the last people to get out, so I'm pretty good.

We do lots of fun stuff at the afterschool place. We even got to watch Star Wars and Return of the Jedi when it was too hot to go outside. My favorite day was today. We made real ice cream, all sugary and creamy with crunchy ice—I could even taste the vanilla! It was *so* yummy! I want an ice cream machine, too. The one we used was metal and cold, and stayed cold even though we were making it outside, underneath the burning sun. Tomorrow I think I'll make something like a necklace or picture frame like the other kids are doing. But not all day. I like the exercise from playing games outside. I'm already as tan as an almond and my hair is as yellow-white as a peeled banana.

I do a half-cartwheel as I run to Mom's car, my hair falling not so gracefully on the sidewalk. It slides back into position at the base of my spine as I stand upright and listen to Mom's lecturing about being "lady-like."

Around the neighborhood...

My stomach jumps to my throat as I set off again, risking skinning my knees, elbows, and face as I yearn for the thrill of gliding down the cemented hill. I close my eyes. The exhilaration of flying fills my heart. I pretend that the screeching of my metal skates are mystical birds or sounds of a plane.

I'm out of control. I wobble, my arms flail wildly and I try to steady myself, but I crash onto the rough sidewalk. I get up and try again.

In the front yard...

The smoothness, sweet and sugary, is replaced by sandpaper roughness. It tastes like sweet metal in my mouth. I see red on the half-eaten jawbreaker. I swallow the blood in my mouth and keep going. I have to win! I ignore the numbness and swelling and continue to lick the once sweet candy.

"This is boring. I'm going home." Danny gets up to leave. I pause in shock, jawbreaker in midair, mouth hanging wide open.

"En I win, right?"

"No."

"Yeth I do! I win becauth you quith! I win!"

"Whatever."

I'm furious. Danny gets up and walks away. I look down at the troublesome candy. I lost my taste buds soon after my tongue started bleeding and all I can taste now is the blood on the unhurt taste buds on the side of my tongue and mouth. Maybe if I rinse off the candy and wrap it up and put it in the fridge, I can finish it when I can taste again...

In the kitchen...

My eyes start to twitch from fatigue—I think—until they refuse to focus and my gaze is forced upward and the wall moves down as I fall, again. This time somebody sees me and it's too late to run to my room, not that I'd have the energy to move my legs anyway. So I wait for my body's panic attack to go away. Through strobe vision I see Dad looking down at me with a horrified look on his face. I feel embarrassed and ashamed for the first time about falling. *What's wrong with him? He looks scared. I feel fine, just take off my glasses and let me sleep it off. When I wake up, I'll only have a headache and a bump on my head.* My mouth opens to say these things, but all I hear myself say is a croaky "*daddy*." *Oh, great. I've freaked him out even more.*

They later tell me that I have a disability. Epilepsy. I don't believe it. Everyone falls down occasionally. Even Sis does. I just do it more often. I feel scared. Does this mean I'm going to die? The doctors tell Mom that they can give me medication to make the seizures go away, but until then, I can't do anything. Everyone's careful with me now, like I'm different. Even after the doctors give me the medication, I'm still not allowed to do anything. *I can still do anything I want! Just watch me!* Now there are rules that I have to follow. I'm not allowed to play on the bars on the playground anymore, even though I do the best flips. That doesn't matter. I have to be safe. Inside. *I can handle falling down! I can feel it coming and I know what to do next, like rest and drink orange juice. I feel like they're taking my life away.*

A month passes. I sit on my bed, looking out the window at the sunny afternoon. *I'm not going to be like those kids out there again. I'm not allowed to do anything. I* can't *do anything.*

Getting baptized...

It's summertime, and I'm getting baptized near the church. I'm in the shallow end of the pool with the pastor and he asks me a bunch of questions like, do you believe that Jesus is the Son of God? I'm glad I memorized tons of Bible verses in Sunday School, but he doesn't ask me about them. Instead he dunks me backwards in the water. I remember to hold my nose so I won't breathe in the water. He brings me back up. Everybody's smiling. I feel so special!

Stuck at home...

Instead of enrolling us in public school, Mom's going to teach us at home. A few months ago I would have been upset. But the teachers and the other kids treat me so differently now, I can't wait to get away from them. Mom knows me. If I don't understand something, I can just tell her and she won't look at me like I'm stupid. Mom says that our public school was going to put me and Sis in Special Ed because they're too stupid to notice that we were having petitmal seizures. That's the kind of seizure where you space out for a few seconds. I thought grownups were supposed to notice stuff like this. They don't care. Nobody knows what it's like. Well, except for Sis. I'm glad I have a twin sister.

Our home schooling lasts the whole day. It helps, going slower. I don't like to rush. Rushing makes me all panicky, especially around people I don't know. My favorite books that Mom uses are the Readers and the history books. I want to travel to distant lands and discover a bunch of new countries, but I think they're all found. Science is fun, too. We do experiments in the kitchen and figure out how things work. The best day is Friday. We have sewing lessons and horseback riding. We go to somebody's house—also a home schooler—and meet other kids who learn at home. I don't like the girl who lives there. She's a real snob. I still have a little bit of fun, though. I'm making a pincushion and it looks pretty cool. It's a tiny round pillow with lace all around the side. It has blue flowers all over it. I get excited when the class is over because then I get to see the horses at the marine stables. Mine is Buck, a palomino. He's not actually mine, but he's the horse that I ride for my horseback riding lessons. At first Mom had us take English riding lessons, but there was nothing to grab onto and I had to ride a certain way. It was just too weird and dumb. I convinced Mom to let Sis and me take western riding lessons instead. It's so much fun! Just last Friday I finally trotted around the ring. My butt always hurts afterwards, but it's so much fun, I don't care. When I get Buck to run, I feel like I'm flying or riding a wave. It's so awesome! Buck likes it, too.

Leaving California...

Mom and Dad decide to move us back to North Carolina. We won't be living on a marine base, though. I hope things will be like they were when we were little. Maybe we'll get to visit Grandma and Grandpop all the time and go to the beach a lot.

I stare out the side window at the cars going by. I *was* getting bored until I started memorizing license plates. I have almost twenty in my head right now.

Through the rear windshield I see...

Twinkling
So small and far away
I gaze at the fading lights
Jonathan
El Toro
"Tako"
Even the beach—all gone
No, I'm the one that's going
I have to remember
I take a mental picture
The bright lights far away
The caked sand on the beach
The brown layer sandwiched between the blue-green ocean and colorful horizon

Jonathan
Handball
Fresh home-made crunchy vanilla ice cream
Tears steal away from my eyes
My stomach hurts, as if to burst forth
Escaping under the car's wheels
I want to go home
It's another adventure, I say
I'm an adventurer
Traveling to exotic places
Solving mysteries and collecting fortunes
By the time I reach North Carolina everyone will know me
I'll have a million friends
Maybe Mom will buy me a puppy

Chapter 3
Back Home

In Pittsboro, N.C....

The house looks a lot cooler than I thought it would be. It reminds me of the cute little brown wooden Lincoln log toys that Sis and I had when we were little. I wish we still had those. They'd still be fun to play with. The house looks so mysterious and solitary, hidden away from the street for about a mile. It'll be a ways to walk and then we'll have to ride a bus, which I don't like to think about because I don't like to walk much and I've never ridden on a bus before. I'm glad I'll have Sis with me.

Our house is also surrounded by trees filled with mosquitoes, crickets, and other strange noises. I know I'll be awake forever at night, but hopefully I'll get used to it and be able to fall asleep. Except for those noises, it's a lot quieter here. And not just because we live in the woods. Since Dad's moved into a trailer, there's no more yelling. Mom and Ram have their own rooms and Sis and I have to share one again. We have bunk beds. I claimed the top and Sis got the bottom. I wish I'd gotten the bottom. Then I could've built my own fort and nobody would bother me while I'm reading. Oh well.

There's this dirt road that I've started to ride my bike on. I pretend that the other houses nearby aren't really there, so it's just us. And I'd be trapped in the woods or some fantasy world.

Sixth grade at Horton Middle School...

It's my first day of public schooling. I'm in sixth grade now and I can barely remember what being in a real classroom is like.

I can't find my shoes! My worst nightmare is coming true. *I'll have to wear my lemon-yellow flip flops. No! I'll be a geek! Nobody will want to hang out with someone in flip-flops!* Stress is overwhelming me. Next thing I know, my head's hit the floor. I can't think straight, but I'm angry anyway because I *do* know that I've had another stupid seizure and I wonder if I can keep from having them at school. *What if no one knows what to do and they send me to the hospital when I don't have to go? What a waste of a day. No one wants to be friends with a girl who wears flip-flops and falls on the floor, shaking all over the place, making weird noises. I want to stay home. Why can't Mom just teach me at home again? If only she was still with dad, then she won't have to work and can still teach me at home. Then I won't ever have to see people stare at me. I won't ever be made fun of and I can just be best friends with my sister and no one else. She'll make lots of friends here, though. She's nicer than me, so everybody likes her. I always say something stupid because I talk too much and always have to be right.* Mom tells me that I'll feel better after lunch, so she'll take me to school then. I don't say anything. *If I don't look at anyone, maybe they'll ignore me. I just won't talk. I hope the teacher doesn't call on me.*

Heart racing, stomach sinking, my throat goes dry as my eyes quickly scan the front of the busy classroom. Everyone is so outgoing. Everyone except me. Everyone seems to know each other. They smile, giggle, and whisper to their friends as the teacher passes by. My math homework sits undisturbed and ungraded in my hands. *Where do I turn it in?* Shy and confused, I slip it shakily back into my desk, my math grade slipping lower each day along with my self-confidence.

The WILDCATS of 4th period...

The stuffy locker room is full of gossiping, giggling girls who are quickly changing clothes for gym class. So far, my other classes have turned out okay. I'm starting to figure out where everything goes and the teachers are really nice to me. Mrs. Williams is my favorite teacher. She teaches English, and lets us write any story or poem that we want. She's also my homeroom teacher and tries to make the new kids feel really welcome and special in this tough place. I've been here for only two weeks and I already have a favorite teacher!

"Manda, hurry up! The bell er' ready rang! Where are ya?" It's my new friend, Tina.

"I'm in here—the bathroom." I'm real modest, as my mom would say. I'm just plain shy. I hate to undress in public, even though we're all girls and we're all in a locker room. "I'll be right out. Don't wait for me." Somehow my foot keeps getting caught on the wrong side of my shorts and I almost fall. Changing in a rush doesn't help matters any. Why does it always take me forever to change?

"Okay." Tina pauses for a minute, hesitant to leave me by myself. Hearing Ms. Ginn's voice quickly changes her thinking, however, and she darts out the locker room, tapping her small feet against the gymnasium floor. After about a minute passes by, I frantically shove my carefully folded school clothes into my book bag, then run out of the bathroom and into the locker room. I suddenly stop dead in my tracks as I realize how loud I am, or rather, how empty the locker room sounds with nobody in there but me. *What kind of excuse can I make up? None. I'm simply late.* "Oh, boy," I mutter and try hard not to imagine the mean look on Ms. Ginn's face. She feels sorry for no one and doesn't accept excuses from anybody. She reminds me of a guy. She has a low voice, yells real loud, has short brown hair, a pudgy-looking nose, and a circular body with muscles. She's aggressive and competitive and expects us to be that way, too.

I'm about to leave, but fear hits me as I wonder why the gym is so silent. I should be hearing bouncing basketballs or volleyballs or at least Ms. Ginn's loud voice. Nobody can complain about not being able to hear her voice, although some idiots sarcastically do.

Cautiously, I peek out of the locker room doorway to the huge gymnasium that proudly has in bold red letters, W-I-L-D-C-A-T-S, on the sides of the floor. In the middle of the floor and on the side of the wall an angry wildcat silently roars at the bleachers. Its menacing face reveals ferociously glaring black eyes and white teeth. Yet there are no little "wildcats" running around.

"Oh, no!" I whisper, as a horrible thought crosses my mind. What if they're all outside? How can they be outside? We weren't there yesterday! I run to the door on the other side of the gym. I squint at the sun's bright glare. It's too bad I can't enjoy the warm weather. As I carefully scan the brick buildings on the other side of the street, a huge field covered with shouting middle school kids running back and forth (obviously playing soccer) comes into view behind the junior high building.

Go on, Amanda, what else are you going to do? Stand here all day? I try to get up enough courage to walk all the way over there, but it isn't working. My class hasn't gone outside before, so I have no idea what to do or where to go. After all, I *am* new.

No, those kids don't look like the ones in my class. That's the junior high P.E. class...I think. Turning back around, I glance at the empty bleachers and polished floor and decide to go back to the gray-walled locker room. *Where are my friends?* I wonder despairingly. I feel totally depressed. Earlier today, one of the guys that I hate saw me accidentally walk into the boys' bathroom and told everybody! I made that stupid mistake right after lunch and in the most crowded place. Anyway, skipping P.E. doesn't seem so bad. What's bad is that I have nowhere to go and no one to go with me.

Squeaky sneakers pound the floor as a little fourth grader in neon pink and dark green grass stains jumps up and down, looking for a bathroom. I hide in a stall and pretend that I have an excuse to be there. Bored after she leaves, I stay in the stall and read the scribbling on the door and sides. *Katy* **LUVS** *Richard.* I take another look. That adorable guy, Richard, in my math class? And my new best friend, Katie? It does look like her handwriting, but Katie spells her name with 'ie', not a 'y'. I read the other messages. I know practically every single name written on here. Maybe I should write something, too.

Loud laughter and groans pierce the air of the quiet room, signaling the end of P.E. class. I decide to stay in the bathroom so I won't draw attention to myself. I grab my school clothes and start to change, too. I wait, listening to everyone else's conversations. The usual loud and intimidating conversations continue while the girls change out of their gym clothes.

"I couldn't believe it!" One skinny, indignant girl cries out in disgust. "Throwin' the ball instayed of kickin' it!"

Her big friend laughs. "I felt like yellin' out, 'Hey, fool, we ain't playin' no damn basketball!'"

"Can you spell s-o-c-c-e-r?" The skinny girl laughs sarcastically. "What an idiot!"

Twin girls in identical red shorts walk slowly in, dragging their feet. The taller twin complains over and over about how mean it is to make people run when they don't want to, how even meaner Ms. Ginn is, and how awful P.E. is altogether.

"I can't breathe...why do we gotta run everyday? Michellia, I'm gonna die..." She dramatically drops to the floor. Michellia, however, must have been listening to her the entire hour because she looks too tired and frustrated to show her concern at the moment. I think her sister's a good actress, but oh well. She miraculously recovers and rummages through her clothes. "Michellia, where my blue socks? Ya know, the real cool-lookin' ones?...Michellia? Miche—"

"I don't know, Keisha! Now will ya quit pesterin' me?!" Their argument continues until two girls from dramatically different cliques enter the room in a huff and verbally attack each other. Tension fills the now deathly silent room. For some unknown reason, kids over here always seem to be looking for a fight.

"If you don't shut that snotty moutha yours, I'm gonna shut it for you!" I quickly grab my stuff and get out of this huge black girl's way. Misty is the toughest, scariest, and biggest girl I've ever seen. Everybody is scared of her. *Wow, she's really tall. Or else I'm really short. Is she talking to me?*

"Oh, yeah right, Misty! Just make me!" yells a girl just as big from across the room. *I guess she wasn't talking to me.* Ms. Ginn walks into the locker room and glares at them both. *Man, she's tough. Maybe she went to school here.*

The talking resumes its normal murmur.

"Hey, girl! Where ya been? Not in here the entire time?" Tina fixes her tiny black braids by closing her barrettes tighter than they were before. She turns and looks at me, waiting.

"Well,...I, uh...uh..." I can feel my face growing red. *Do I have to tell her? I never lie.* "Tina, I—" Just then the bell rings. "Oh, look! The bell! I have English next!" Feeling incredibly stupid, I grab my worn-out book bag and run to my next class. There's no way I'm going to take my time getting to class again.

In the cafeteria...

Katie's been my best friend for about a month and I have to say, she's pretty stuck on herself. But our personalities are kinda the same—we're both stubborn and determined. I think that's why we're such good friends. We match.

So here I am again in the cafeteria, sitting across from Katie. It feels so good to have a best friend that I can talk to about stuff. The cafeteria in this school is so big. It's rectangle-shaped, with the food served on the longer side of the cafeteria. My favorite food is the rectangular pizza that they sometimes give us on Fridays. Even though most kids say that the bottom tastes like cardboard, we all like it anyway. It's so embarrassing to be in the cafeteria because it's so obvious that I'm poor. Even though I don't have to find something to take with me to eat, I still feel poor because of the food card that I get. Sitting with Katie makes me feel a lot better because she's really rich and I don't notice myself so much.

This chocolate milk tastes great. If I could, I'd drink just this for the rest of my life. Katie's bragging about one of her new sweaters. She points to the one she's wearing. Suddenly I get a major giggle fit. I see the cows on her sweater as really funny for some weird reason and spit chocolate milk all over them. I apologize over and over, but she keeps on yelling at me. It's not like she can't get a new one, but I don't dare tell her that. I ignore her. Tomorrow she'll have forgiven me. She always does. She likes me too much to dump me outright.

I just found out that Richard likes me, too. Katie's mad at me, of course. Someone must have told her right away, because it wasn't me. I was going to wait. She's acting so ridiculous. She keeps ignoring me but she'll come around. I mean, he's just a guy and there are tons of cute guys around. Sis likes Richard, too. A lot of other girls do. But they can all have him. I still like my Jonathan in California. I wonder if he still remembers me?

Summer at home...

Sixth grade is finally over! I'm lying on the couch watching Michael Jackson on MTV. What else is there to do in the summer? I only see my friends at school, so I have to make new friends at church just to find someone to hang out with. At first it was fun, just doing nothing. That lasted only a week, however, before I started to get bored out of my mind. I'm beginning to wonder just how many singers are out there for MTV to be showing the same eleven videos.

The boredom doesn't last forever. Mom has to work during the day and doesn't want to leave us alone because of our seizures, so she sends us to a daycare even though we're too old for it. At first I felt totally embarrassed, but now I'm having so much fun! Sis and I look so young, anyway, we blend right in. No one makes fun of us. So far, I've made a ton of friends and we get to act, sing, and create all different kinds of artwork. Most of it's simple crafts, but we also do a little painting.

Secretworld...

Every kid has an imagination. Sometimes even an imaginary friend. But when you have a twin, you have a best friend for life. Sis and I made up Secretland when we were bored one day. Secretland is the capital of Secretworld, a place where there's a land for everything. It's located at the center of the Earth and Americans are always sending in spies to dig up all the secrets in this world. Sis and I make up characters that we role play. We use our favorite names. When we change our minds on what our favorite names are, we take the old names and call them our sisters. So far, we have Jean and Jane, Heidi and Heather, Rachel and Michelle, and Alison and Irene. Then we added the name Crystal Peace because it sounds pretty. We all have the same enemy—Kathy Kober. I wanted to add Jonathan as my boyfriend's name, but Sis wanted that name for her boyfriend, so we came up with "John" for her. We travel to exotic places, encounter trouble, and think of interesting ways of escaping and getting rid of the bad guy.

Down the dirt road to the street...

Fudgie was sold to us as a Yorkshire Terrier, but she looks more like a Silky. She's small, dark, and square shaped, just like a piece of fudge. We try tying ribbons in her hair, but she's too tomboyish to keep them in. Her favorite pastime is running around the house between meals. I don't think she ever takes naps. Like most doggies, Fudgie follows us when we go for walks.

Mom let us invite Katie and Keara over. Keara is Sis's best friend. I talk to her most of the time while Sis talks to Katie. I'm relieved that those two are hanging out right now because Katie's really been getting on my nerves lately. Keara's really sweet. We're all walking down the dirt road that leads to the street where the school bus usually picks us up. Keara and I are still on the trail, talking about seventh grade. She doesn't seem as nervous as I am and her sense of humor cheers me up. I drag my feet a little to keep some distance between us and the other two. I don't want Katie to run back here and interrupt us with her nonstop jabbering.

Katie's not jabbering, though. She's yelling. Sort of. I think she's upset. Sis is telling us something, too. Suddenly I realize that Fudgie isn't barking anymore. Wasn't she with them? But they were by the road!

"Come on!" Keara turns me around. "They want us to get help!" We run toward my house. *It's too far away. I'm running out of breath. I can't run this entire way. We're doing this for a dog?* I feel horrible. *I love Fudgie! Then why do I suddenly feel like laughing?* Keara and I look at each other and laugh. At the same time I know what we're both thinking: 'I don't want to cry, so I'm going to laugh.' It's hard to hold anything in when you're running.

I don't look at Fudgie when they bring her back. I sneak a peek at the shoebox and see some fur all messed up. But I look away real quick. No wonder Sis and Katie are crying. I feel bad for laughing earlier, but I'm still glad I never saw Fudgie die.

Like our other unfortunate pets, we bury Fudgie in the shoebox in the front yard. I can only imagine what the future owners of this house will think if their dogs ever dig up all these bones. I hope their animals don't freak out.

My first novel...

Good news! Even to cheer up Sis! Today is our birthday—May 26—and now we're twelve! Mom got me a typewriter because she knows how much I like to write. Usually it's just poems because I don't have enough space in my notebooks to write a book. I want to write a book by Christmas. That's seven months away, so I better get started. I'm going to write every single day. I have a writing desk to put my typewriter on, too.

I've been reading tons of Trixie Belden mysteries. I like her tomboyish attitude. Plus she gets to live on a huge ranch and have her own horse. She always sticks her nose where it doesn't belong and faces tough bad guys. I've decided that I want my book to be a mystery novel. I'm calling it, *Secret of the Hidden Treasure*.

At Church...

Mom stopped going to church. I still want to go, though, and so does Sis. Actually, I just like doing all the fun things that we always get to do in youth group. Like sleepovers at the church, or retreats. There's a beach retreat coming up. Everyone will be going to the beach! I just hope Mom will say yes. It's going to be so much fun!

Mom said yes! I was so happy then and I'm even happier now! My new friend, Debbie, isn't as burnt as me. I look like a lobster. I love the sounds of the ocean, the smell of the sand and the salt sprayed from the water into the breeze. My senses grow stronger when we get closer and closer to where we are staying. I'm so glad I came! Debbie is such an awesome person! She has medium brown hair that's just long enough to pull back into a ponytail. Most of the time it's loose and flat, and sticks to her face. Her glasses look like mine. Her dad's a preacher, so of course she has to be somewhat of a brat, but only in a way that says—*what I say goes, so don't even think of pushing me around!*

We decide to go to the mall and get our picture taken from one of those black-and-white picture booths. I smile my usual goofy grin that's on a too-wide face, showing big front teeth and brown glasses that are slipping down my nose. I'm definitely going to try to remember everything about this retreat: the time I'm spending with Debbie; the fun time I'm having trying to learn how to play volleyball (even though my competitive attitude always ruins everything—I have to work on that); the meals we eat in the mess hall; and yes, even the long walks we take to get to the pool.

Too soon it's over and I'm on the bus heading back home. *This stinks.*

Oh, wait! Finally something funny! A really cool memory I'm adding about the bus ride home is Austin's perfect imitation of UB40's Red Red Wine.

Starting junior high...

I guess I'm a bit *too* sure of myself. I thought Katie was my best friend—someone I could count on if I needed somebody to talk to or hang out with. But she's dumped me for Ashley and Julie, the snobbiest girls in school. We used to make fun of snobs like them. I think she was just pretending to be friends with me because she was new, too. But because she got those popular girls' attention, she's now popular, too. They're rich, too, so of course it had to end up this way. Now that I think about it, I can see why she doesn't want to be friends with me anymore. I think we're *too* much alike. We both always have to be right. Maybe she felt left out of our club of friends. I'm the president and I make up all the games. What did she get to do if she couldn't be the leader? We both wanted that spot. I guess Ashley and Julie make her feel included, what with them being rich and stuck-up and all. I still feel really mad. I hate Ashley and Julie. How can Katie be such an idiot? Is she really as stuck-up as they are? No, I know she brags a lot, but she's still a nice person. Someday she'll be in my shoes and she'll know exactly how I feel.

I'm glad I'm not like Katie. People are friends with me because I tell the truth about how I feel about them. Plus, everyone says that I'm a happy person and everyone likes being around happy people.

The youth group's Winter Break...

It's wintertime and everybody's talking about trips that they plan on taking soon. Right now the youth group is talking about a really awesome retreat to a ski resort in Wintergreen, Virginia, but I don't think Mom will let me go. Maybe if I do a bunch of nice things for her and ask her when she's in a good mood...

The first day we're only supposed to practice doing "the pie" down the bunny slope. It looks so easy when everybody else does it. I want to strangle Lindsey. She's getting on my nerves. Why can't she just ski with another group if she's so good? I fall way too many times, but I still plan on going down the highest slope. It looks so cool! And so much fun! I get up to the top and breathe in the fresh air, adjusting my hands on the poles to get a good grip. I push myself forward. I can feel myself flying down, but it feels like I'm going too fast. *I'm not paying attention to my legs!* Somehow I wind up skiing backwards and then slide sideways into a prickly bush. *Some joker must have thought it would be real funny to plant prickly bushes here and bet on how many unfortunate beginners would run into them.* I finally reach the bottom of the slope. I'm practically crawling on the ground. Luckily my youth group forces me to go back to the hotel for dinner. Otherwise I would be twisting around the mountain all night, just to get it right.

I was going to practice going down that slope again today, but this morning I met David Italian-something. He tries to show off by naming all the hotels that his dad owns in the area and then he offers to buy me dinner. Of course I say yes. I tease him mercilessly, but let him teach me how to ski. It feels good to sneak away from my group and eat dinner with a guy. I return to the hotel and ignore the lecture from my leader. I agree to spend the rest of the weekend with the group. The next morning I hurry off to meet David because he said he'd buy me breakfast. I bump into my group that afternoon. They tell my friend Lindsey to keep an eye on me. She bugs David by constantly babbling and simply existing. So while we're on the ski lift, he decides to tell her of the many "accidents" that occurred in the very same chair we're sitting in. She freaks out and leaves us as soon as we reach the other side. I laugh and we talk about school and our homes until it's time for me to leave with the rest of the group. It was a great weekend! Everyone in my group, especially Sis, is upset at me for ditching them, but I had so fun on that man-made frozen mountain that I don't care. I had a great weekend.

One last look at the Lincoln log house...

I'm kicking myself for throwing it away. I'm not going to write another mystery because this one—*Secret of the Hidden Treasure*—was so bad, but I still think I should have kept at least one copy.

I'm so stressed right now! I'm not sure how I feel about moving to Colorado. Ram won't be coming with us. He's going to live in the trailer with Dad. Colorado sounds like fun and I hear it's beautiful, but I don't know anybody there. All my friends are here. Still, I like adventure and moving to a snowy home in the middle of nowhere sounds kinda cool. I just hate the moving part. Couldn't we get moving people to lug around all this stuff? I feel dizzy. I'm half-listening to Mom.

"You'll like it there," I hear Mom saying. "He built a house for us, with your own room and a loft. The land in Colorado is beautiful. The school is a lot better than the one here. Since he's the bus driver, there won't be anyone starting fights on the bus." She looks pointedly at me.

"Brad started it! He kept calling me and Sis names!"

"Let's not talk about it."

It was sorta true. Brad kept calling us 'nuns' because of our long skirts. We're short, so most of our clothes are too big for us. So I got back at him by drawing a picture of him with a pig nose. I must've hit a sensitive nerve because he demanded that I give him the picture. Logical request. However, something clicked inside of me and I gave him an "I dare you to mess with me look." I snidely said no and threw the picture on the floor underneath me so he couldn't reach it. He leapt on top of me, then put his hands on my throat to try to choke me. I was actually surprised and not very upset or worried that I was losing my breath. I tried punching his chest, but it wasn't working. He was still on top of me. Eventually the fight was broken up before I had a chance to pass out. I got sent to the principal. I tried to look as innocent as I could, but he must have been used to it because his face revealed nothing. I found out later that Brad had been in fights before, so he got kicked off the bus, whereas I got sent out with just a warning.

"Bring out the black and white TV from the living room, will you?" Mom's voice shakes me from my day dreaming.

"I'm not done with my stuff yet." I run back to my room and just stand there. I really like this Lincoln log house. My room looks so cool. The window across from my bed, next to my writing desk, shows the forest behind our house—trees with hanging branches that for some reason always look wet. My imagination would run wild as I pictured the forest coming to life, acting as guards against the intruders that yearned to pass into the glorious kingdom I knew lay beyond. I grab my glass bowl of shells off my dresser, remembering how long ago it was when I started collecting them. *Colorado doesn't have beaches. When's the next time we'll even get to visit a beach?*

I carry the shells outside. All of a sudden I feel very ill. I try to convince myself that I really am looking forward to the move. But leaving Keara, Tina, Eddie, Ram…

I open my eyes. I'm on the ground, with Mom bending over me. My head hurts. *My shells!* I look next to me and see them scattered on the ground, most of them broken, mingling with shards of glass. I find five shells still intact and Mom says we can put them in Sis's bowl. She says that she doesn't mind. Mom takes me inside to rest. I was feeling depressed, but now the only thing I can think of is how relieved I am that I have an excuse not to help with the move.

I gaze at the plastic landscape outside my screen door. A slight movement catches my eye, but nothing is different. Only the leaves of the changing season. Fudgie, once circling my heels for attention, lies unmoving underneath the patted dirt in my front yard, along with two pet mice and two birds from the past two years. Our last animal never had the chance to join our pet cemetery. He was returned to the same animal shelter that we took him from.

We move on to more scenic landscapes.

Chapter 4

Crispy Winters and Hickish Places

In the middle of nowhere...

It's nice. Colorado is really beautiful. The whole sky is painted with different colors at sunset. If it weren't such an isolated place I would want to stay here. Here, in a colorful desert place with white crispy winters and where it's easy to breathe. If only we were closer to town—what a small, neat little place! Turquoise jewelry, feathered trinkets, and blankets with wolves on them that are made by interesting people! I love the restaurant with the staircase and balcony, where I can go to the top and look at all the people without them staring back at me.

Ignacio, Colorado...

Today was different than most days. At school we now have an extra 30-minute class called IAM. Mrs. Moody is my assistant teacher for that class.

My schedule at school starts with English. There's this absolutely gorgeous guy named Brian who sits in the back. He's tall, with black hair and looks so much older than everyone else. Of course all the other girls in the school like him, too, so I don't stand a chance. Besides, I think he likes the girl up front. Her name is Sarah. She has brown hair and looks older than everybody else, too.

Next I have Band. No one cute in there. J.J. is a real brat, but Sis is in my class, so I can ignore him.

Third hour I have Mrs. Federico, my science (earth) teacher. One weirdo who swears and mumbles to himself sits next to me. Yuck!

Fourth I have History. The teacher's monotonous voice could lead anyone into the world of insanity. Jason, the guy who sits on my right, teases everyone, including me. Robert, who sits on my left, talks too much.

Then comes lunch. We sit with two seventh graders, Sarah and Elizabeth. They're our friends, too.

Fifth hour is Keyboarding. Jason and Robert are in that class. And so is this one cute seventh grader, Brett. I know he's one year younger than me, but give me a break!

Sixth hour is the best. Communications. We make the yearbook, school newspapers, and letters to parents. But the real reason why I like to be in there is because of Todd. The guy that Sis, her friend Sheana, and I like. So does our enemy, Heidi. She is *so* stuck-up! But she's also pretty. Todd's the sports editor and Heidi videotapes the school games, so they get to spend a lot of time together.

Seventh hour is Pre-Algebra. It's so easy; it's one of my favorite subjects. This adorable guy named Dustin sits *right behind* me! He's so *gorgeous*!!!!!

Colorado

Surrounded by the vastness of the desert, I embrace my solitude. There is no loneliness I feel, no boredom as the earth touches my feet, no irritation as the dust in the air tickles the back of my throat. The sky in the afternoon is the same sky everywhere, so I wait. I close my eyes and thoughts. I hear lizards scuttle across the clay ground, yards—perhaps miles—away. I don't remember missing the ocean or the dense green sprawled over North Carolina. Instead I smell dirt and I'm alone in a world where one can die unnoticed, unbothered, in peace. I want to scream. To stay. To have been born here perhaps. This desert is now my home. I bask in its beauty. Its dryness. Its solitude. Its myths. The sky turns pink. Purple. Red. Orange. The mountains reflect the colors back to the clouds and suddenly the sky tears apart. Heaven peeks through. The world is ignited with a beautiful illusion of colors. I watch. It doesn't fade. I blink. It doesn't fade. My mind wanders. It's gone. The colors have disappeared behind the mountains. Tomorrow I will not be distracted and the colors will stay.

Running to the Midwest...

I must have written at least a dozen twisted nature-oriented poems while I lived in Colorado, but I lost them all when Mom told us one day to pack all our things. The guy we had stayed with turned out to be strange in a possibly dangerous sort of way. Mom had us pack everything quickly into the car while he was gone and she hasn't looked back since. I wish I could do the same. It was so pretty out there, I was inspired to write the best poems I've ever written.

I tried to convince myself that our home in the desert was too quiet; too far removed from civilization. Growing up in the desert would be too weird, anyway. I was finally relieved when we left the state. That is, until I came here to South Callaway, Missouri.

Lost in Backwards Country...

It's the most backward and hickish place I've ever lived in. I've never done so many chores in my entire life! Mom, Sis and I are staying with a family whose norm is getting up at 4 a.m. They do tons of chores, eat, and then the boys take the bus to school. They have no girls. When we get home, we have to pitch in with even more chores.

The school is so small that there are only four extracurricular classes: Art, Home-ec, Band and Choir. I have to take three. Of course I'm sticking with Band, but there's no way that I'm ever going to take Home-ec., so I decide to take Art and Choir. Art is so much fun! I can get an A for scribbling, this class is so easy. The Band teacher is pregnant and seems to show up only when she feels like it, which is just about never. We still practice the music that we have. No one skips. I don't know if that means we're good kids or complete geeks. As for Choir, I mouth all the notes. I don't know what a 'C' is supposed to sound like. Most of the time I sing by ear and talk to the girl next to me. She tells me about her older boyfriend with a truck and what sex is like. I'm totally shocked. I keep telling her to dump him; that she shouldn't even be thinking about sex at thirteen. I can't even imagine kissing a guy. She says the boys our age are too immature. I keep reminding her that hanging out with best friends is way better and much more fun than hanging out with any guy. Even though she agrees with me, she's still with him.

I hate leaving her, but my next class is P.E. I'm learning how to play floor hockey. I'm finally having fun! I'm vicious. Well, not really. But I'm fast and I finally like a game that's team-related. I like playing defense. *Just try and get past me*!

The hour flies by and too soon it's time to change. I always skip the showers. I'm not about to shower in public, plus we only have a few minutes and I always take a long time. I dodge the perfumes the girls spray. It stinks up the bathroom, but the girls seem so sophisticated. I want to try wearing some, too. I borrow some from my friend. I use it like she tells me to—put some drops on one hand and rub it on my neck, then do the same with my wrist. I feel older and sophisticated. I glide to the lunchroom with a smile on my face. I notice excitedly that some people are turning their heads in my direction. I walk up to Sis and her friends.

"So, what do you think?" I'm grinning as I put my wrist to Sis's nose for a whiff. She jerks her head away.

"You better wash that stuff off. It stinks. People are starting to talk."

"But it's perfume! Isn't it supposed to smell like this?"

"I hope not!" One of Sis's friends interjects. Sis ignores her and continues.

"Whoever loaned you that stuff forgot to tell you that the perfume has to go with your body chemistry in order to work," she tells me in her usual practical tone of voice. "Otherwise it smells like that."

The people who had turned their heads before are still looking at me. *First she tells me to call her Angela instead of Sis, and now she embarrasses me in front of everybody!* I quickly run to the bathroom and wash off the perfume, telling myself never to wear this crap again. If I want to smell good, I'll just take a long bath with scented soap.

My first boyfriend...

I'm sitting at the movie theatre next to Jeff—my very first date! I'm more annoyed than excited, however. I turn my head and see Mom and Sis giggling at me from the back row. *Let them look. At least I'm the one with a real date.* Jeff doesn't notice how nervous I am, probably because he's too busy being nervous himself. *Geez, his face looks so tense.* I look up at the movie screen and see why. It's the beginning of Look Who's Talking, where sperm are racing to an egg and the main character is conceived. And I thought health class was embarrassing! I want to melt in my seat, but the twisted, sarcastic side of me decides to torture my adorably nervous date by staring at his cute profile, making him blush. I forget about my Mom and my sister and escape into the movie.

Jeff was so shy that *I* had to ask *him* to go with me to the dance a few weeks later. I don't mind, though. I have a date! Mom drops us off and I'm relieved that she doesn't follow us in. His friends stand off to the side, laughing at us, but unlike them, Jeff is dancing with a cute girl—me! My favorite slow song, with the sexy saxophone in the background, is playing. I melt into Jeff's arms. Everything is so romantic, so perfect, even though my date is dancing like a robot. I'm sure the song ended and I went home, but everything went all dreamy after that first dance.

Finishing up in Fulton, Missouri...

Mom decided to move us to Fulton, Missouri. The school here is much better than the last one! I'm still thirteen and still in eighth grade. We moved in the middle of the year. Since the math taught at the hick school was so easy, the one at this new school is extremely difficult. My teacher considered holding me back, but Mom fought and won. My favorite class is P.E. We play floor hockey, just like at the other school. Jenny, my new best friend, is our goalie and just as bad as I am, but we still brag about having aggressive skills and quick maneuvers.

Today Jenny invited me to her new house. She shows me all of her favorite metal band posters. "Don't you think he's gorgeous?" she asks, drooling over one particular poster on her door.

I laugh. "I can't tell. He's glaring at me."

I finish eighth grade in that school and even get a junior high graduation ceremony. All the kids think it's lame, but I like the attention.

Meeting my baby brother again...

Mom just met someone and I had hoped that wherever he took us would be someplace nice, like the beach. I found out that it's not the east or west coast or any place as beautiful as Colorado. We're still stuck in the Midwest. Our next destination—Moline, Illinois.

"He should be here any minute now."

Mom's excitement is rubbing off on me. My baby brother Ram, who's been living with Dad all this time is coming to live with us. It was different not having those two around the house. Quieter. Ram will get his own room, being the only boy, but I don't mind sharing a room with Angela. In North Carolina, we would stay up talking long after Mom said "lights out." Most of the time I would hide a flashlight under my bed and take it out at bedtime to finish reading the Trixie Beldon book I had to set aside that afternoon to do homework.

Ram is coming. How old is he now? Let's see, I'll be fourteen in a few weeks and I'm seven years older than him, so he's seven? Eight? In any case, Mom said that he's starting third grade in the fall. Once we're "settled" in Illinois. I hope it's better than here. I'm so bored! But the fair should be fun. It's in a few days and Mom says that we'll meet her fiancé then. I hope he's nice.

"He's here!" Angela's looking out the window and Mom's already downstairs, passing a few disgruntled neighbors in the hallway. *It's a good thing we're moving. It's too small here for four people, especially if we're gonna need another room for Ram.*

He looks so much bigger than the little toddler I remember, and a lot quieter. He still looks small, though. And really nervous. I hope I don't look nervous. I should act like a big sister.

"Hey, Ram! How'ya doin'? Here, let me take that." I grab his suitcase and shove it on Angela. "Angela, hold this." I walk down the hallway and head up the stairs, occasionally looking back at Ram. "Ram, you're gonna love it here. I mean, it's a little boring, but there are tons of kids to play with, as long as you're not too shy. Watch your step. There's not much to do, but we're moving to Illinois, anyway, and I think Mom said it'll be different. Yeah, Mom said we'll have a stepsister, too. I hope she's not weird or annoying or anything. Did you bring anything fun to play? We have Scrabble somewhere—what?" Angela's saying something. "Oh, we don't? We must have lost it in a move then, but that's okay. Whew! There are a lotta steps here! We have Monopoly and I know how much you like that." I stop at the top of the stairs, with Ram standing two steps behind me. "Mom, unlock the door. Oh, I feel stupid. It's already unlocked." I feel dumb for rambling, but I can't stop. Luckily, Mom hands me something to do before I can open my mouth again. Things will definitely be weirder from here on out.

The big blue house in Moline, Illinois...

The house in Illinois is nice. Angela and I share our own room again upstairs. We have a new stepsister. She has her own room. She's going into seventh grade and acts extremely shallow and a lot less mature than we ever were at her age. The wedding is held in the living room and Mom looks so pretty. She's wearing a simple yet nice dress. I feel a lot happier now. Mom's happy. We have a real family. Mom said that we'll be going to Moline High School, which is supposed to be much better and safer than the other schools around here. I push the thought of high school out of my head. I don't want to think about that huge place right now.

Chapter 5

Dreams and Death

A new stepsister...

I'm fourteen and she's eleven, but it might as well be the other way around. My new stepsister, Jill, looks like she's in high school. I'm treated like I'm in elementary school. It's not fair, but as long as everyone leaves me alone, I'm fine. I have my Sweet Valley High books, my daily devotionals that uplift me and inspire my poetry, and my walkman. Every night I used to listen to Def Leppard until I decided one day to switch to only Christian music. I'm told that developing a new attitude of "only Christian everything" will keep me out of trouble and into my writing and homework.

Emily...

It's in the afternoon and I'm in my writing room studying "Acts." Suddenly the cutest gray kitten that I've ever seen is placed on my Bible. I squeal in delight. Her blue eyes widen in terror and her blue-gray body cringes in fear. She positions her paws to dart into the hallway when she's seized by unknown excited hands. She's pulled closer to the loud oohs and ahs. "You're just the cutest wittle kitty

kitty, yeshoo are!" Her ears perk back and forth as the hands scratch them from behind and stroke her tiny head. Ram decides to name her Emily after a little girl that he likes.

Little blue-gray calico Emily.

Two weeks have passed and she's grown slightly. At least that's what Mom keeps saying. *Where is she?* "Emy...Emily...! Come here, kitty, kitty!" I look everywhere. Nothing. "Mom! I can't find Emily anywhere! I've looked everywhere!" We look again.

"She'll turn up somewhere."

She gives me chores to do. Grumpily, I reach into my closet for my dirty clothes. Emily squints at me from the laundry basket.

Do you mind shutting the door, please? I was sleeping, but now I'm wide awake, no thanks to you.

"Emily! Ooooh, my little kitteee..."

No, don't pick me up...don't pick me up!

"Okay! Okay! Fine! Stay in the dirty clothes basket. Mom, I found her! You'll never guess where she was!"

Drama at MHS...

I probably shouldn't take it. But it looks like so much fun and Lonnie tells me that I can take it if I want too, that Mom won't mind—I doubt that—and he says that I'll do well in whatever class I take.

Well, Mom *did* say yes, and now I'm having the time of my life! Drama lets me be whoever I want to be. Today I play the role of Junie Moon, a co-dependent woman whose boyfriend burned one side of her face. I get up in front of the classroom and sit in the chair that's facing the class. My heart's pounding, even though I don't need to know any lines. It's simply learning drama. Right now we're learning facial expressions. I pretend that I'm sitting up in the hospital bed. I look around, trying to get a grasp on what has happened. When memories begin to surface, I slowly touch the right side of my face. I flinch in terror because I know that what's there isn't very pretty. Filled with dread, yet at the same time extremely curious, I pretend to take a mirror that I find in a drawer next to the bed. I close my eyes. I hold the mirror up to my face. First the left side. I open my eyes. I look very tired. I move the mirror to the other side, perhaps a little too quickly. I gasp. I gingerly touch my cheek with the other hand and start to cry. I drop the mirror on the bed and cry into my hands. My dramatic tears wow everyone in the class and I receive an A for my performance.

It's several days later and we're being taught improvisation. We're given characters and a situation. We don't need a plot just yet. Three others in the class and I are lost in the woods. I'm a pretentious snob. I complain during the entire journey and make sure everyone knows how miserable I am.

Another skit. Only this time we make everything up—characters, lines, and the scenes (must be short). In this one, I'm a spokesperson for a cereal commercial where I convince the audience of the cereal's nutritional value while the taste tester passes out behind me. My favorite character that I've played so far in the other scenes is the airhead. I enjoy making other people laugh at my infuriatingly empty-headed expression. I understand the art of projecting one's voice, but I have yet to master it. I feel like I'm going to sound like a chipmunk forever. I'm going to train my voice to speak lower.

So far, I've conquered my fear of standing in front of people by fully throwing myself into my character, and it's turned out beautifully. I keep getting A after A, so I think I'm going to brave an audition. I want a role—any role—I don't care, so long as I'm in it. Right now, the play is Up the Down Staircase. It's set in a school, and most of the characters are either students or teachers, so it shouldn't be too difficult an audition.

I know she's out there, watching me. I can hear her booming voice. *She* has no problem with projection. My drama teacher is also the director of our school plays. So the good thing is, even if I don't do well in the audition, she'll remember how good I am in class and hopefully she'll keep that in mind. It's hot underneath the spotlight and I can't see the audience. I feel like I'm at one of my Band concerts, only I'm standing up and without a uniform.

I walk on the stage completely nervous. I act out the first few lines, trying to remember all at once everything I've learned. *Speak loud, but don't shout. Always somewhat face the audience so they can see you and hear your voice. Look several lines ahead, occasionally glancing at the paper, but look around and act the part, don't simply read the part.* My nervousness makes it difficult at first, but I catch myself several times before I make too many mistakes. As I read the lines, I change into a completely different person. I let my character take over. By the time I walk off the stage, I'm smiling confidently, holding my head high, and mentally going through all the mistakes I made and how I could have done a better job.

I'm glad I decided to wait in between classes to look at the callback list. I hate crowds and I'm too short to look over people's shoulders, anyway.

I stand next to two girls: one of them a nice popular girl—a great actress—who grins excitedly. I don't recognize the other girl, who glares at us both and struts away. I scan the list for my name, only slightly nervous. *Why would I get a part, right?* I remember that only popular kids get parts in plays. Or maybe they're popular because they're in plays. Or maybe since they're a part of everything else, naturally they'd also have a part in a play. Or maybe—*There I am!* "Amanda Melot…Extra." I squeal and then scream inwardly as a few kids glance curiously at me. I look back at the list. "Melot"—*Arrrrgghh! Are they ever going to spell my name right?* I really don't care. I'm in a play! I jump up and down, this time oblivious of anyone around me. The late bell rings. *Two tardies—one more and I'll get detention.* I quickly grab the wrong books from my locker and run happily to German class.

My favorite opera...

I'm so excited! Our teacher told us that we're taking a field trip to Chicago to see Phantom of the Opera. I have no idea what it's about, but the idea of going somewhere on my own and feeling so included in a cool group leaves me dizzy with excitement! Mom says that we don't have the money. However, after a bit of juggling, I find myself in the windy city, in a building carpeted in red velvet and other fancy décor. I don't care too much about looking out of place. Soon I'm listening to the opera (I can't see anything and I can't afford binoculars). The woman's sweet notes and the Phantom's spine-tingling deep voice hypnotize me. The voices are so mesmerizing that I don't pay much attention to the story. By the time we reach the bus I feel so romanced, I'm in a world all my own. I melt dreamily into the seat next to my boyfriend Aaron as we ride the bus back to the school. Those around me are laughing and talking, but all my robotic boyfriend wants to do is sleep. He's sitting numbly next to me, facing the window with his back to me. I decide to inch my jean skirt up a little. I lean against his shoulder, trying to look as cute as possible. Nothing. He doesn't even glance in my direction, but instead shrugs me off of him. *I should have asked out Adrian. At least he's cute and interesting.* But he was too shy and avoided my advances. Aaron was available and interested in dating me and I wanted a boyfriend. I guess Aaron isn't really interested in me after all. Why is he dating me then?

A week later, Angela hands me the phone. It's Aaron. I'm so excited! Two more days until the dance!

"Hello!" I yell into the phone. Aaron tells me that he's not really interested in going to the dance. Would I rather go bowling, instead? Shocked, I burst into tears and hand the phone to Angela. She tells him how horrible he is for making me cry. I love my family. It works. He changes his mind and agrees to go.

I shouldn't have raised my hopes. I'm standing next to my locker at school, tempted to crawl inside it and die. Aaron's talking to me and I don't have Angela or anyone else to stick up for me. I feel so stupid. I don't want to cry, so I just keep nodding my head and go along with it. I, being too polite to take a shoe and shove it up his butt, agree to ditch the dance and he walks away. I'm labeling this as our official breakup because I plan on ignoring him from now on. I deserve better than a "convenient" boyfriend. I'm not going to the dance. Even if I could go with a guy friend, I wouldn't. It just doesn't feel right. Guys are stupid. Girls are much more fun to hang out with.

In freshmen English...

It was in Mr. Collin's class that I decided to become a writer and a high school English teacher. He's a writer, too. I found this out when we had to do a book report for the class. After I got my paper back, I realized that he was the author. It's my favorite biography, *George Washington Carver*. He was the man that invented the many uses for the peanut. I'm not a brown-noser because everyone likes Mr. Collins, and he likes everyone, so it's not like I've become teacher's pet. He's a good teacher and has us read books that I've never heard of before, like *Contender*—about a boxer struggling to make it—and my favorite, *The Game*—a twisted story about survival, where a hunter's guide realizes that the game has turned on *him* and now *he's* the prey.

Today we're supposed to spend the entire period writing something—anything—and then hand it in at the end of the hour. I stare at a blank sheet of paper for what seems like an hour. Twenty minutes have gone by and I still can't think of anything. Well, not anything interesting, anyway. Some of the other kids in the class are also staring at their notebooks in sheer desperation. Others are scribbling furiously. A few boys are simply sitting back, waiting for class to end. I wonder if they've actually written anything. I think I'm the only one looking around. I better pay attention.

A picture pops into my head. A bunch of kids running around, all different, each with something to say. I'm good with rhyme. Ten minutes go by quickly and I'm done. I sit back and smile, reading the finished product and occasionally editing, clipping and adding as I read.

Darrell, Who Had Dropped the Bell

Laura laughed as Francis fell
When Darrell dropped the booming bell.
Julie jumped out of her seat.
Randy raced to catch her feet,
But Betsy bumped into the boy
And they both tripped right into Troy,
Who then plummeted into Pammy.
"Such a silly scene!" Said Sammy.
Ricky roared with such laughter
That Lily laughed and Dan dove after
Missy, who had made the mistake
Of giving Greg the bell to take
To Darrell, who had dropped the bell,
And everyone around him fell,
Except for Kate, Dave, Jon, and Tess.
They had escaped from the big mess.
Tess, today, still tells the tale
Of Darrell, who had dropped the bell.

Unfair advantage...

I bet I'd like my biology class much better if Mr. What's-his-face wasn't my teacher. He's such a jerk! He's like one of those characters you see on TV or hear about in other people's stories about their families or acquaintances. He isn't even middle age—mid sixties is more like it, yet he drives a bright red sports car and hits on every young woman he meets, including my Mom. Never his students, just teases the girls. But that's not why I think he's such a jerk. He has an annual tomato contest, where everyone grows their own tomato plant and whoever has the tallest plant wins. He handed out the seeds in class and told us the rules. He took out his "secret ingredient" that helped him win every year. As soon as I saw the familiar blue liquid I yelled out, "I know what that is! That's Miracle Gro, isn't it?" Mom uses the same stuff on her plants at home. I never should have said anything. My teacher gave me a mean look. I grinned. The class laughed. That weekend he said he'd look after everyone's plants. So far mine was the tallest—I had been using my own "secret ingredient." Monday came. At first I couldn't find my tomato plant. Then there it was, hiding behind a whole bunch of others. Off to the side. And almost dead. It looked like it had been suffocated. I was tempted to strangle my teacher and his winning plant, but the tomato was innocent and I was sure my teacher would die soon anyway from bad temper overload.

Johnny Angel...

It's dated Wednesday, September 12th, 1991. I'm totally surprised. After all, the last letter from Jonathan was in eighth grade. That was a year and a half ago! What made him want to write to me now? I carefully open the envelope—I want to save it—and curiously open the letter and read its contents. First he went to Pennsylvania for basketball camp. Then he spent the rest of the summer on a mission trip to St. Lucia in the West Indies. They ran a Vacation Bible School for the island kids. He wrote an article describing his experience that was published in a magazine for teenage guys. He attended another teen leadership conference afterwards. By the end of the summer, he had made the decision to attend seminary school after high school graduation and become a pastor.

He goes on to describe his schedule for sophomore year: geometry, world history, English II, chemistry, band, French III, and marching band after school.

I read the words that are scribbled next to the article: *Have you grown any? I am now 6'4" and 190 lbs. Write back soon!* I then read the enclosed article with a dreamy smile.

At Wharton Field House...

I'm climbing up the bleachers to play with the pep band at a basketball game when I discover to my embarrassment that the other school's pep band is playing, not mine. Mom's already dropped me off at the Field House, so there's nothing I can do but wait. I feel so stupid in my glaring maroon and white striped jersey, standing on the wrong side of the field house among the opposing fans. To my relief, I spot a couple from church, Mr. and Mrs. Schafer. Mr. Schafer's going to sing at half time. He's pretty good. He's a Christian singer with an amazing voice and already has several tapes out.

I'm having a great night until I get home and tell Mom about my night. Then I get to the good part, when Mrs. Schafer and I sat together and talked while Mr. Schafer sang at half time.

"His wife was there." Mom interrupts in a loud voice, looking at the redneck as he enters the room. She isn't asking, she's stating it, as if to mark it as a fact.

Did I miss something?

"She's lying!" He roars at me. He gives me a menacing glare. Like I care. Only Mom's lectures and yelling have ever had any effect on me. Unnecessary yelling from any other adult is simply annoying and judgmental.

Mom looks at me. "Are you sure it was his wife that you saw?" Under their gazes I suddenly feel unsure. *I think she said she was his wife. What if I'm wrong?* I take one look at the redneck and make my decision. "Yes, I'm positive it was Mrs. Schafer. I talked to her the whole time. She's really nice, even bought me nachos. Why?"

Mom continues to stare at the redneck. "You said you went to the Amway convention this weekend with Lonnie's wife *and* Mrs. Schafer. You lied."

"You're taking her word over mine? She hates me!"

"She's not the only one!"

I go off to bed with a knot in my stomach. I hate being in the middle of an argument, but knowing that God's using me to trap that jerk in a web of his own lies makes me feel better.

I can't bring myself to be happy with our new family. Sure, I get a huge bedroom and a side room where I can do my devotions and a kitten called Emily and a piano in the dining room downstairs in a beautiful big blue house, but Mom gets the rotten end of the bargain. She deserves better. I promise that when I publish my first book, I'll buy Mom the houseboat she's always wanted with room for all the funny looking plants that she likes.

Lonnie...

Jill's dad—the redneck—has a best friend named Lonnie. Lonnie's opposite him in every way: a good father, loving and faithful husband, an obedient and sincere Christian, genuine, kind, and completely selfless. Whenever someone needs help, he's there. He taught Angela and me how to shuffle, play solitaire (which is now my new addiction), and helped us register for ninth grade in our new school. He even believes that if he, Angela and I sit down together and pray earnestly to God to take away our seizures, He will. We did that and it didn't work, but I've learned one thing—if genuine love and concern is all it takes, our seizures would have disappeared the moment God heard him utter those words.

A few months later I'm thinking about Lonnie as I walk in the door, half expecting Jill's dad to greet me by saying something unintelligent and insensitive. I notice Mom first because she's crying. Jill's dad's face is sad. Usually he's what everybody else calls "charming." All I see is an overly friendly redneck masking what I believe to be obvious stupidity.

Mom's the one to tell me about Lonnie. He was at work—he was an electrician—and one tiny piece of his hair touched a bare wall, wires exposed. The electric shock threw him across the room and he died instantly.

Something hits me in the gut. Is it disbelief? Everyone seems to be waiting for some kind of reaction. *What do they expect? I don't want to cry. I don't think I can even if I tried.*

Loneliness creeps into my stomach. He was twenty-nine. When Jill found out, she sobbed hysterically and everyone made sure she was okay. Now she's saying that she wants her friend—Lonnie's wife—to marry her dad "so they can be like sisters." She never liked Mom.

A lot of odd things kept happening after Lonnie died. His parents hired a detective to see if his death really was an accident or if it was some form of foul play.

Anyway, Mom, Angela, Ram and I moved into a shelter downtown, the package of us wrapped tighter than ever.

I totally flopped on my finals. It's the middle of my junior year and everything seems to be hitting me all at once. I even got a B on my German final, and I've always gotten straight A's in that class. I flunked the P.E. final and got C's in Geometry and Consumer Ed. I feel so trapped! I can't even tell my friends where I live! I feel like a huge shadow is squeezing my heart. Nobody understands me. But as long as I have school to go to, I'll be okay.

Mom found a trailer that's right next to the Super Saver Cinema! It's small, and Ram still gets his own room while Mom, Angela and

I have to share one, but I feel so much better here. Even though Ram's totally annoying, I'm glad we're all together. Just us. We're back to our real family again.

Sweet sixteen…

It's in Mom's name, but to Angela and me, the paper route still feels like a real job. We split the route and our paycheck between us. I wanted to apply at Whitey's Ice Cream, like most of the high schoolers, or the Dunkin' Donuts in front of our school—most of the kids that migrate there still leave clouds of smoke by the door even though a law was passed that makes it illegal to smoke within 500 yards of the school—but I would have to work until late at night and Mom's afraid we'll have seizures from lack of sleep.

Each customer on the paper route is different. There's the lady who saves every single Christmas card she receives and posts them on her living room wall every Christmas. There's the nice old artist who once painted landscapes and owns an old shaky dog named Lady. There's the mean old lady who yelled at me for getting her paper wet because I had slipped on the ice and hit my head. What I like best about the paper route are the paychecks. I feel independent. I go to the Super Saver's Cinema at least twice a week. And when Aladdin entered the theatres, I saw it four times—one time with Angela, and three times alone. I like watching movies in the theatre by myself.

Youth for Christ…

Angela and I started going to YFC (Youth for Christ) at our local church. It's sort of like a youth group, only we're borrowing the church for our meetings, and instead of the church kids meeting together, kids from all over the Quad Cities can get together to talk about God and get to know Him better, and we also play games. I met a cute and really nice guy named Jeremy there. The leader warned me against hanging out with a guy like him because he's from a rougher school and all, and he thinks Jeremy will pressure me into doing "certain things." I guess he thinks I'm a completely innocent person that doesn't think any lustful thoughts. It doesn't matter, because both Jeremy and I are all talk, which makes for interesting and stimulating conversations.

Once we decided to go to the YMCA with my friend Heather. We played keep-away in the pool. Heather had a crush on him, so when I suggested to her that we gang up on him, she agreed. I tried to jokingly karate chop his leg when I realized too late that water slows down movements and I missed and hit something a lot softer than his leg. He wasn't feeling too good after that. I'm glad we're still friends. I wasn't sure we would be after seeing the look on his face.

My heart's pounding as Jeremy and I tease each other. I know I can beat him at wrestling, but I think I'll go ahead and let him win these rounds. I like it when his long brown hair falls across his face, brushing mine. He's so cute!

Mom doesn't like it when we make too many phone calls and the trailer isn't a private place to carry on a conversation, so I usually wait until Mom goes shopping at Aldi's, and go with her. She takes forever, so I call Jeremy from a payphone and we just talk about everything under the sun for at least an hour. We always tease each other about nothing in particular.

I still don't know about asking him out. I like what we have now better. I don't want anything to change. For two years I've thought that his eyes were brown. Then when I brought this up in a conversation he looked at me weird and told me that they were blue. I feel dumb. All that time we were wrestling and staring into each other's eyes, and I didn't even notice. I hope he isn't too insulted. After all, I don't think it was his eyes that I was paying attention to.

After a while of tolerating my endless teasing, Jeremy fell for someone who went to his school. I loved teasing him about her because I enjoyed watching such a "tough" guy fall head over heels for a pretty girl. I didn't see him much after that, and when I did he acted weird—aloof and "tough"—around me. So much for male-female friendships.

The missionary...

I received another letter from Jonathan. It's dated August 15th, 1992. Last year he sounded too busy for any long distance friendships. I open his letter. It's a lot smaller than the last one, probably because there's no thick article included with the letter like last time. He thanks me for the autographed Al Denson poster that I sent him. Al Denson's one of my favorite Christian singers and I know that Jonathan really likes him, too. I was able to get his autograph when he had a concert at my high school. Jonathan tells me that he attended an annual youth conference in Wisconsin with his youth group. They spent a week ministering to people with special needs. The last night they were there, their pastor surprised them with tickets to a Steven Curtis Chapman concert. He's another Christian singer. Jonathan tells me about basketball camp, a teen leadership conference at a Bible college in Pennsylvania, and working at Vacation Bible School at his church. He casually informs me that his mom has breast cancer, then moves on to the next subject. I wonder how he truly feels about his mom's situation. I really doubt that he has absolutely no worries whatsoever, no matter how faithful he is that God will come through. I stop and say a quick prayer for him and his family. He goes on to complain that in NJ (where he lives right now), the law states that one has to wait until they're seventeen to get a driver's license. Then he tells me that he got Reggie White to speak at his Bible club at school. I never heard of him, but Jonathan says that he's a famous football player. Then he writes, "*Al Denson called me yesterday!*" My jaw drops. Jonathan had left a message two days earlier asking if he could perform a concert in his hometown. The secretary said that he'd call him back. Jonathan thought, "*Yeah, right!*" But Al Denson actually returned his phone call! Jonathan would still have to raise $5000 total. Knowing him, he'll accomplish that feat, no problem.

Jonathan leaves me with Joshua 1:8 and a school picture of him grinning with his head back in confidence.

A little music in the trailer...

I feel so tired. I walk into my room and set my backpack on the bed across from the door. Suddenly I see the cutest little canary sitting in a little cage on my dresser in the corner. Mom pokes her head through the door.

"Mom, I love you!"

"I thought you'd like him. Now don't forget to feed him."

"I won't."

"He's your responsibility."

"I know. I'll take good care of him. Hey, little birdie! Hey, look at his feathers—"

"Tiny animals are very fragile. You have to remember to feed him every day."

"I know Mom, I will. You don't have to keep on telling me."

"I just want you to remember how important—"

"I know. Look at his feathers. He's peach-colored. Isn't that cute? Aren't canaries supposed to be yellow?"

Mom leans over my shoulder, studying the bird. "I think so, but he's perfectly healthy."

"Good. I'll call him Peach."

"That's nice. You might want to feed him before dinner."

"Okay."

My new little friend keeps me happy with his music, especially when I get too stressed out over my never-ending algebra homework.

I just got home. I'm excited to be with Peach. I decide to give him some extra treats. I take his food, about to pour the seeds into his trough, when my hand slightly bumps the cage. I'm about to apologize when Peach, standing next to his dish, falls forward on his beak and remains in that frozen position. My stomach drops and my heart feels pierced by my selfishness. I fall on my bed and cry myself to sleep as Mom quietly disposes of Peach.

I had forgotten to feed him.

The feeling of slow motion…

I wake up on the floor in band class. The florescent lights are bearing down on me. I squint. *My head hurts. I must have had a seizure.* My pants feel wet. *Oh, no!* I see my teacher peering down at me, an expression of concern and guilt on his face. He probably thinks it's his fault for yelling at me or something. The last thing I remember is being in the middle of a giggle fit when I was supposed to be playing my flute. All the kids crowd around me. I start to get upset. I don't want their sympathy or have to answer any dumb questions. I just want to change pants before anyone notices that they're wet. *It's all my fault.* All of this could have been avoided. I'd been feeling dizzy the whole day and as usual, I kept ignoring the signs.

I'm too weak to stand on my own, so someone helps me into the office. I sleep for the rest of the hour. When I get up, I feel much better. Unfortunately, I probably won't get to skip the rest of my classes and go home.

My last high school performance...

It's the beginning of my senior year and I sit miserably with a bunch of freshmen. Our band performance is over. The symphonic band—made up of upperclassmen—performs Phantom of the Opera. It's full of sweet and slow songs, unlike the band performance two years ago. They had played allegro-filled songs that were also from Phantom of the Opera. One song included a scream given by one of the flutists. It was awesome. This year's symphonic band is still good, but not as good as those talented seniors before them. I watch and listen as they give it their all without me. I watch my friend Shelly expertly finger all the notes, much faster than I ever could. I should have chosen a different instrument, maybe one that concentrated on beat and rhythm and not so much on style. Like the drums. I've always liked them, but in sixth grade they weren't something that a girl would play, and I wanted something feminine.

A few days later, I'm standing three feet away from my band teacher's office door. It's gonna take everything I have, but I'm going to march in there and tell him exactly what I want. I'll demand that he let me march with the rest of the seniors in the marching band. It's enough that he kept me in the freshmen band, but to not be recognized with the rest of my class? I don't *think* so! I burst into his office, smile nervously, then politely give my rehearsed speech—*I've been in band all through high school, and even though I'm not in Symphonic band, I feel it's extremely important that I be announced along with the rest of the senior class.*

"Sure. Just okay it with your fourth hour teacher and then come here to practice marching."

I'm shocked. He's letting me march? No argument? Before he changes his mind, I quickly agree and leave. The only thing I won't be allowed to do is march to Hang On Sloopy. Somehow it worked its way into becoming the senior's song. We love it. It's a complicated elephant formation, but I still wish I could join them. At least I get to march to the school song.

I can't play my flute very well and march at the same time, so I fake the playing and concentrate on the steps and turns instead. Who's gonna notice?

I feel so proud on the marching field while I play the cheesy school song (I have it memorized now). After forming into a giant 'M' for Moline, we stand silently as someone announces the names of all the seniors. I hear my name.

"Amanda Mellott."

They pronounced my name right! What a way to end the night.

Chapter 6

Lost in the Eye

Illinois State University...

I'm surrounded by education majors and a bunch of booths that are strewn about the gigantic ballroom in the Bone Student Center. Preview can be summed up in one word—pamphlets. There are pamphlets everywhere! Information on secondary education, elementary education, special education, general education, teaching college, and even pamphlets on teaching teachers! First I have to take a bunch of required general classes, and then I have to take classes for the English part of my major, and also classes for the education part of my major. There are tons of classes I have to take in order to get my teaching certificate. I feel totally overwhelmed. A slight panic sets in. Where do I begin? What if I forget a class? Can I possibly finish all this in only four years? It all looks so complicated and difficult!

I look at the other freshmen in the room. They look so confident. I feel like the only person who doesn't know what the heck is going on, or what to do next.

Suddenly a pink face surrounded by a million red curls jumps in front of me. She's really friendly and I'm relieved that someone's finally talking to me. The only problem is that I can't understand what she's saying. She's talking way too fast! I say "what?" a few times, feeling more and more rude. I get an idea. I point around the room, then at my ear and mouth the words, *I can't hear.* She starts to speak slower. I learn that we're both education majors. I feel more sure of myself. It doesn't matter that *everyone* in the room is an education major. Someone has finally decided to give me the time of day! She tells me that she's majoring in special education. I start to feel uncomfortable. I never know how to act around people with disabilities or know what to say to them. I can't relate to people in wheelchairs or mentally challenged people. Except that I can't drive, I feel like a normal healthy person. Melissa doesn't give me a chance to respond. She's now telling me her life's story as we travel around the room. Once again she's lapsed into speed talking, but I'm catching on better. I tell her about Ram and Angela, and she tells me about her younger sister who is still in high school. I discover that we have a lot in common. We both like drama and absolutely adore cats!

By the end of the night I not only understand her, but we're talking at the same time as well! We plan on getting together soon and she's going to introduce me to all of her school friends. For a freshman, she sure does know a lot of people! We exchange email addresses and then she goes home. I'm so excited that I forget how lonely, scared and overwhelmed I felt when I first entered the room. I wonder if Angela has met anyone at her preview for art majors. I want to introduce Melissa to her. And to Mom. I told Melissa that Mom, Angela and I are all going to school together. Now that Mom is an anthropology major, she's going to be spending most of her time in Edwards Hall. It's a pretty gray building with ivy hanging all over it.

I pick up a few pamphlets on my way out of the building and pass by the Bowling and Billiards Center next door, by the parking lot. Maybe Melissa and I can go there sometime. I study one of the pamphlets and stop in the middle of the parking lot. *Join the Illinois Shakespeare Festival at Ewing Manor this fall!* I don't know where Ewing Manor is, but the picture looks really cool! The place looks like it was taken out of medieval times. The audience is set up in a semicircle around the front of the stage. The manor is the backdrop and partial stage to the three performances that are held there. The whole area is in a courtyard, with tall trees surrounding the old manor.

I have to show this to Angela! Mom would love this, too! I walk quickly out of the parking lot and down the Constitution Trail until I see a set of apartments off the trail. I run inside our apartment, nearly tripping over our new puppy, Arthur. I begin to describe everything at preview, speed talking to whoever will listen.

Artie...

It's Artie's first birthday. He's so cute in his little party hat! I hold up my disposable camera. *Snap!* The little Cairn terrier smiles up at me as our Pomeranian puppy, Hendrix, runs in circles around the both of us. Artie's trying to look cute, so I'll give him a piece of vanilla cake from the pan that I'm trying to place on the counter that divides the kitchen from the living room. Hendrix runs into the back room—Ram's room—and returns with his stuffed chicken that he had left in there. He does this when he wants to go outside. Hendrix looks like a rat trapped inside a giant cheese puff.

Artie continues to gaze up at me with those big brown eyes. Mom puts leashes on the puppies and takes them outside while simultaneously carrying an armful of water balloons. I smile as she hands a blue one to Artie. To my amazement, he picks it up carefully, and without breaking it, he struts around the yard with his present. *Snap!* Hendrix, on the other hand, is having no such luck. The yellow balloon that Mom gave him pops in his face before he has a chance to pick it up. *Snap!* He seems to like the water, however, and soon he's popping the balloons on purpose. I look at the front porch. No more water balloons left.

I listen to Mom tell the story of when we first got Artie. He was even smaller than he is now. One time he was walking on top of the couch when all of a sudden he disappeared. Mom leaned over the back of the couch and saw Artie between it and the wall, looking around in bewilderment.

Four more pictures left. The birthday cake! *Snap!* There was only enough frosting to spell out, *Happy b-day Artie!* We give Artie and Hendrix each a piece of cake. *Snap!* They wolf down their frosted treats, and now it's time for their nap. Artie happily enters his crate. He lies on his side as usual, and his eyes catch mine through the bars of his prison. *Snap! Snap!* He falls asleep.

Sophomore year…

The phone rings. It's Melissa. She tells me that she met a fellow online and they talked about pretty much everything. Then out of nowhere he suggested that they meet in person. She reluctantly agreed, but she doesn't want to meet him alone. So she decided to call me and beg me to join her, just to be safe. I'm curious, so I say yes.

We meet at the Coffeehouse, sit down, and introduce one another. I can tell that Melissa feels really uncomfortable. The fellow, Matt, briefly talks to her, then turns his attention to me after she makes it clear that she's not interested. He seems to like me. Unused to the attention and flattery, I gobble it up.

It isn't love or infatuation that prompts me to say yes. I feel flattered to be noticed at all. Most guys never give me a second glance. I'm happy to follow Matt everywhere—his apartment, his mother's home—and hang out with him and his loud and obnoxious buddies. I spend most weekends with his family. The first weekend I visited them it was his sister's sixteenth birthday. I met his Mom, her boyfriend, and his sister. She's rebellious, intelligent and a very good storyteller. I totally like her. Her family gave her goofy presents, but I surprised her with an Italian-made silver necklace. It cost a lot, but it was worth it to see her drop her guard and unmask a look of surprise and delight. I figure every girl, no matter how tough she acts, sees age sixteen as a magical age and a major step into womanhood.

Even though it's been only two months, Matt and I are engaged! The proposal wasn't very romantic, though. I had proposed in order to mend an argument. But we're happy now, and he bought me a pretty little ring with a tiny emerald on a tiny gold band. It's so cute! I can't wait until the wedding! Mom and I picked out a dress. Since we're having a renaissance-style wedding, we got a simple white dress that was made in India. It didn't cost much, but it's really nice. It has three thin layers, each one longer than the first. I don't know where we're going to have the wedding yet, but I'm pretty sure we want it outside.

There are some things that are surfacing that are really starting to bother me. One of which is his sense of humor. It's extremely condescending and makes me feel stupid and insignificant. Even though I have Matt wrapped around my finger and I know that his friends like me better than they like him, I still feel unimportant and useless.

I really enjoy wearing my beautiful ring, but this relationship is emotionally wearing me down. I panic when I think of how he's controlling the relationship. My independence and freedom feel removed, as if they're merely band-aids on a wound that he'll soon remedy. Plus, I'm a strong Christian and he's agnostic. I don't want my future children to grow up in a non-Christian home.

We're sitting in a small booth in one of the dorm's cafeterias. My heart is pounding. *It's either now or never.*

"Matt,...I..." *What? I think we should break up because my Mom thinks you're a jerk and I'm just now beginning to see that she might be right? No. Too harsh. Although...he* did *get drunk at a party and kissed one of the girls there. What if he does that again? If he was a Christian, he never would have gone for the party scene in the first place.* And *he'd treat me with a lot more respect.*

I sit up straight. "I don't want to marry someone who's not a Christian. There are just too many issues that would come up and tear us apart. And I wouldn't change my stance on any of them—"

I hold out my hand to stop him from speaking as he opens his mouth to object.

"—I know you told me that you'd convert so I'd marry you, but you can't do that. I mean,...someone either believes or they don't. You told me that you were agnostic, so how can you all of a sudden decide to change just because I want you to? You can only change if *you* really believe. So I think we should just break it off."

I hand the ring back to him.

I didn't want to hurt him, but I can tell that I had. Nothing I can do about it now. I will *not* back down. I quietly excuse myself and leave the table. By the time I'm safely outside, I can feel the weight I carried with me for two months melt away. I feel free and a little guilty. But only a little.

I'm back to my usual routine. I wonder if the relationship had been worth it. I've certainly learned what kind of guy to avoid, but what kind of guy do I really want? Do I really care if someone writes me poetry and flatters me constantly if at the same time he's bashing my self-worth?

Living with Mom on Lincoln Street...

With Matt out of the picture, I have plenty of time to study. However, I'm getting more and more stressed out with each passing day. I'm constantly running out of money for food, and the added stress of loneliness that I feel when I go to my cliquish Christian organization at school each Thursday night is causing my seizures to increase to about twice a week. I get so groggy that it's really hard to concentrate. I'm not going to give up, though. The only time I actually considered dropping out of school was when I got engaged to Matt. He was going to support us both. I feel so stupid now. What was I thinking? He wasn't even in college! How would we have paid for my medication after we got married and I no longer received my medical card? Oh well, that's over with. Now I just have to survive today. These seizures aren't making it any easier. They're becoming more dangerous as each one lasts longer. Since I don't know what goes on when I'm having a seizure, I had to learn from Mom that my seizures are becoming more violent, and occasionally I even stop breathing.

I need a 2.5 GPA to stay in the education program. I'm buckling down hard to raise my current GPA of 1.8. Since I had neglected my studies to spend more time with Matt, I failed that semester and fell into academic probation. I'm trying not to panic. There are plenty of easy classes I can take to help raise my GPA: art, band, pep band, a couple of literature classes and maybe even a history class.

Mom convinced me to switch medications from Phenobarbital to Depakote. My seizures are lessening. I have decided to stop attending that Christian clique and join my sister's Christian group instead that's run by the students. I've noticed that the members' genuine attitudes extend also to their love for God and concern for the other people there.

My GPA has increased to 2.0! I'm feeling better every day!

The Possum...

I'm on my way to the bank to take out some money for Cheetos and iced tea. I need a debit card! I'm walking through the quad and notice a cute guy studying on the grass. I turn my head and see something that makes me stop in mid-step. Some strange looking creature is several feet in front of me. It's staring at me in the same manner that I'm staring at it. I turn to the cute guy and ask him what kind of creature this animal is. Smiling at me (he must have realized that I'm not from around here), he tells me that it's a possum. I continue to stare at the possum, admiring its uniqueness. We stare at one another. After a moment we cautiously circle one another, and then go our separate ways. What an interesting way to start off a morning!

What I get from writing...

Why do I write? English teachers always ask the same questions. I stare at my empty sheet of paper, twisting my face in concentration. I pretend to have tunnel vision by blocking out the other students in the classroom from my mind. I focus on the tip of my pencil. I find words that describe my feelings and scribble them down.

Sometimes I just want to write how I feel, maybe portray it in a story. I don't expect it to be great because it's not intended to be read by anyone but me. Most of the time, however, I like to write for others. I want to write stories that make people laugh, think, or just be able to relate to. Writing stories for others is one of my biggest thrills. It's also one of my biggest fears. What if nobody likes it? Then all my hard work has been in vain and I'll feel like a failure. But the happiness I feel when I see someone caught up in one of my stories pushes me on.

In Downtown Normal...

I was talking to my best friend via telephone, and she arranged for our group's usual dinner get-together at a tiny new restaurant downtown. It's one of those places that's constantly changing. We decide to eat there before somebody turns it into a health food store or another gamer's store. Our group isn't that big, but we still have to squeeze around two tables that we join together. Jeff has to duck underneath the doorway. Funny thing is, I'm not exactly sure when I first noticed him. I mean *really* noticed him. I remember sitting with my friends, slowly relishing a $.50 bag of Cheetos and reminding myself to cherish this moment because it won't last forever. I'm not a pessimist, just a realist. Maybe even a romantic at times. Everyone will eventually graduate or transfer, leaving me alone with my cherished memories. They'll probably wonder why I'm still near the university when everyone else I know has already moved on. I listen and laugh with them, glancing occasionally at Jeff when he speaks. I wonder whether his voice is naturally that deep or if he's speaking in that tone simply to impress everyone.

I don't really know what to make of Jeff. Is he someone I can see myself dating? He's too quiet, too into computers, too tall, has dark blond hair that's too long and a nose that's too big. And do I really go for the rugged type anyway? Then I wonder what it would be like to kiss those heart-shaped lips.

A few weeks later I pass by the bus stop next to his dorm and hear him call my name. It's one of the few spontaneous things he's done since I've known him. He looks like he's not sure if he's saying hello to me or my sister. My stomach does a double flip. I'm actually surprised. I didn't realize how much I wanted him until I heard him call my name. It's been a year and I keep convincing myself that I don't want to date him because he isn't a Christian. I cave in anyway and ask him out via email. He says yes!

The Zipper...

Jeff's finally taking me somewhere other than a food place on campus or to Capen Cinema, also on campus. I get excited as I zigzag through Navy Pier. All the rides beckon to me. One in particular catches my eye. The Zipper. I am definitely not going on that! A few minutes later Jeff and I are climbing aboard. I'm totally tense. *Why am I doing this? I'm going to freak out!* Somebody drops the padded bar over me. I'm locked in. *This can't be good. I have no control now. I'm stuck. Maybe if I close my eyes...* As the seat moves upward, my stomach plummets. The seat rocks dangerously up, my body tipping backwards. My stomach is not pleased. I imagine the seat coming apart, carrying me across the park and into the icy water. We climb to the top (which, by the way, seems to be taking a really long time). Panic enters my head, ripping my thoughts into fragments. *Up up rock rock rock flip upside down rock rock rock rock rock flip again oh my stomach up rock up flip my stomach heart lungs at the top going down fast sharp sideways flipping zipping through the air upside down through the air into space I'm screaming turn my head to look below to see everything as tilted as me my stomach flips with the Zipper we stop.* Someone lifts the padded bar and I unbuckle my seat belt. I stagger out. I think Jeff is standing next to me. I'm not sure. I look back and see another eager rider take my place. *I think I'm sure I think that this yes this Zipper is my favorite ride.* I race to the back of the line.

Horsemen...

I'm in my Greek mythology class with Jeff. The professor is showing us some slides. The slides are interesting, but as the professor goes on and on describing each one, they start get boring real quick. *Horsemen.* Boring. He moves on to the next slide without saying anything.

An ancient Greek temple. The professor tells us a story of a contest. It sounds so ridiculous but interesting. He moves on to the next slide. He talks about Athena.

Slide after slide goes by. My mind wanders. I imagine myself in those times. I'm a Greek warrior. Or better yet, a queen. I hear the professor say something about potbellies. What is he talking about?

I clear my mind to pay attention to what he's saying, but he's already moved on.

A beautiful woman. She reminds me of Virginia Woolf. She's a good writer, and I actually understand her! He moves on without talking about her.

He tells another story of a suicidal manic-depressive. Poor guy.

Another temple.

I hope my braided bun doesn't make me look like a prudent schoolteacher.

A temple with pillars shaped like female statues. Cool! Maybe they're of Athena. Pericles said that an Athenian woman meant nothing. What a jerk.

Another temple. It's beautiful, with round pillars and surrounded by shadows. What did he say about Megara? My mind must have wandered again. I never did get to see Hercules.

A person with no face. I guess that happens to antiques. On solid marble, though? Sculpting marble must be difficult. I bet Angela could do it. She's gotta be the sweetest sister ever. I always feel like the evil twin compared to her. Why does there always have to be an evil twin?

I hope this bun doesn't make me look dumb. Jeff is wearing black again. He's not even taking notes—he's reading a book! He should be listening. I wonder what he's reading.

What a strange bronze sculpture.

Jeff moves his arm away from mine. Why did he do that? Doesn't he like being next to me—don't you, Jeff? You hate my hair, don't you—don't lie.

What did the professor say?

"A sculpture of an enormous ass." Everyone laughs. He's so funny. I like this class.

Family drawings.

Sculptures.

Coins. They look familiar, like the foreign coins I have at home. Why does he keep showing the same one?

Stop reading, Jeff! It's rude!

A pretty pot. Is that of a murder scene? Oh that's pleasant.

The art gets more detailed as the years pass by, but the stories are still the same. Like my hair.

A warrior woman! All right! Oh, no wait—that's a warrior man.

A funny wide drinking cup for parties. It's designed with images warning against too much drinking. Kind of like a warning label. I laugh at a picture of a child's drinking cup and Jeff gives me a questioning look.

I think I see a fairy.

My pen leaks again. I hate this pen! Now my beautifully painted nails are all marked up. I'm being too shallow. Jeff lets me use his pen.

The lights come on and Jeff wants his pen back. I should have taken more notes. Why didn't he let me keep his pen? I'll fix my hair later.

Melissa...

The most fun we had—or at least I had—were the times I'd talk and you'd talk; both of us chattering away and still hanging on every word the other said. We'd watch Friends on Thursdays, have Seinfeld marathons, and talk all night long. I'll never forget how you opened my eyes and my heart. I remember how shy I was the first time you took me to Theatre of Ted hosted by the students every Saturday night. Soon we were regulars and made a lot of new friends, including Henry. I still haven't gone on stage yet to read any of my poems, and I probably never will. You and I used to laugh about guys, relationships, and parents and agreed that none of it made any sense. Do you still feel this way now that you've met someone new? I remember you telling me how I neglected our friendship while I was dating Matt. Now I know how you felt. I left you with an imaginary friend.

Halloween...

I've decided to do something different with myself. Something drastic! I've had long hair for as long as I can remember. I've always wanted it auburn. Melissa looks gorgeous with her short curly hair. I think I'll cut mine, too!

I bring home auburn colored dye and give it to Angela. She's pacing around the bedroom, studying the box of dye. "Okay, I think I've figured out how to do this," Angela says, silently reading the directions. I turn on the tub faucet in the bathroom. I swish my hand around in the water.

"I hope this is the correct temperature. Does it say it on the box?" I look over her shoulder. Angela's standing between the bedroom and the bathroom. "You know the price of having it done is outrageous!"

I'm not sure how much time has passed with my head craned over the tub. It feels like forever. Too bad the sink is too small to use. Brownish-orange dye mixes in with the water and slides down the drain. Some of it stubbornly refuses to move and settles on the bottom of the tub, away from the faucet. I hope it doesn't stain. Angela is saying something, but I can't hear her over the running water.

"Okay." Angela lifts my head and hands me a towel. I look up at her as I wrap my head, but she's just a blur. She hands me my glasses. I get a feeling that something is not quite right. She's too quiet. I put my glasses on. She has this 'oops' look on her face. I look past her into the mirror. It looks like Angela smeared pumpkin guts all over my hair.

"Noooo!" I moan.

"I'm sorry! At least it's all one color. I'm sure it'll fade eventually."

"I thought this dye was supposed to make my hair reddish-brown!"

"Well, maybe your hair's too light." Angela holds up the box. "I told you that when you picked this up." She points at the bottom. "See? Preferred for brunettes." She sets the box down and plays with my hair, as if trying to find a strand that isn't too badly damaged. "But you know, Amanda, I think that once this tones down a bit, it'll look really pretty."

"Really?" I stare in the mirror at the orange mop on my head, trying to imagine what's in Angela's mind. It doesn't look too bad.

"Really." She responds sincerely.

I sigh in contented resignation. "I guess it could have been worse."

Angela smiles. "Yeah, it could've turned green." We laugh. She straightens suddenly. "I know! It's October. You can say you did it for Halloween and dress up as a tree or something!" We laugh some more. I feel much better. I wanted to do something drastic, and I did.

Pumped up, I take the bus to the mall the next day and get my ears triple pierced. *Boy is Mom gonna flip!* A few weeks later I show up at Melissa's Halloween party dressed in my tight green stretch pants and a green turtleneck. Last year I dressed up as a witch in a boring costume. This year I'm a sexy tree-girl!

Speedy Edward...

Today I caught a glimpse of a small brown blur shoot across the floor against the wall. I shriek and stand on my toes like the woman in Tom and Jerry. I jump high as he darts around the room. I hate the sight of him! At least the blur of him, anyway. He moves his legs so fast that I can't get a clear look at him. Angela has a maintenance man set traps all throughout the apartment.

I walk out the door and head to my first class. I imagine the little mouse heading toward one of those death traps. I feel sick to my stomach. Do I really want to extinguish my tiny new roommate just so I can keep my own space? I can't concentrate on the lectures. As soon as I finish all of my classes, I run all the way back to my apartment as fast as I can without passing out. It turns out that Angela was feeling the same guilt all day, too. She gets rid of all the traps and we both feel better. We see a blur speed across the room. We smile. I decide to name him Speedy Edward. Angela likes the name, too. Edward sounds noble.

The next day I return from a long day of three boring lectures. As soon as I walk in the door, I see Angela's face and immediately know that our little friend is gone. For good. Angela tells me that earlier today she heard a loud *snap*. She must have missed one of the traps. She got rid of Speedy Edward before I came home so I wouldn't have to see him. I'm so grateful. Angela is so thoughtful. She knows me really well. I'm not sad for too long, though. Cute as he was, I no longer feel creeped out at night as I wonder if he might dart under my bed sheets while I'm sleeping.

My first Christmas party...

At first I just wanted to cut my hair to about shoulder-length, but then I figured if I'm going to make any big changes, I might as well do them all at once! So I got a perm, too. Not too curly, but with a wave and right above my shoulders, but not too short. It's now just short enough to render my scrunchies completely useless except as wrist ornaments. My hair is still orange from Halloween, but it's faded to a lighter, more tolerable color. I love the changes I've made to my hair!

It's closer to Thanksgiving now than Christmas, but I want to throw a Christmas party at Angela's and my apartment before everyone goes home for winter break. I want everything to be perfect for my party. I make jello shots, buy a plateful of Christmas cookies and then pile a plate with crackers and small chunks of cheese. Now, what should I wear?

The party is absolutely fabulous! Some extra people show up—a friend of a friend, that sort of thing—but it isn't too crowded. I'm a little toasted because I slurped up most of the jello shots. I love jello! There's cherry and orange and some others...I'm dancing around—I feel great! Everybody is smiling at me. Wouldn't it be funny to put my lampshade on my head? I try it and see if I can move around without bumping into anybody or anything. Someone takes a picture.

My mind tells me I'm hyper, but my body disagrees. People are heading out the door. The three foreign exchange students I invited thank me for the fun party and leave. Actually, I only invited one, but she invited two others. I hear a few close friends of mine call my best friend "superficial." I'm really upset and I want to defend her, but in my drunken state I'm not quite sure whether they actually called her that or if it was just my imagination. Or maybe I'm trying to justify my not defending her because I don't want them to dislike me and talk about me behind my back, too. Those are my last thoughts before drifting off to sleep somewhere in the apartment.

The end...

I run from building to building, my mind one giant fragment. My mind isn't slipping—it's melting. I've spent so much time on my senior thesis that I can't think anymore. I'm almost done! I still have to study for tests and finish writing the papers and useless little homework assignments the professors like to throw at seniors before they walk off campus for good. What a thoughtful goodbye.

I can't wait any longer. I have to graduate soon or I'll scream! Maybe it's the anticipation. Or perhaps it's the dizzying rush of other students buzzing around me that has me on edge.

I can't believe it's almost over.

I remember how scared I was when I first got here. Then again, I've always felt that way when I started a new school. At least my nervousness and feeling out of place wasn't foreign to me, like it must have been for some of the other freshmen. All those seemingly impossible years, and yet I never felt like quitting. Except my sophomore year. The year I met Matt. The year I got lazy and almost gave up. I remember thinking, *What's the point? If I drop out now, everything will be easier. Why do I need college anyway? It's not like I'll be able to get a job anyway. I already have a high school diploma. Matt said he doesn't mind if I quit. After we get married, he'll get a job and take care of me for the rest of our lives. Problem solved. This is as close to happily ever after as I'm going to get.* Then when I decided to wise up the seizures started again, as if taunting me that I was right to think that I couldn't make something of myself. Mom took control of the situation, just like she's always done, and got me on a new medication. She helped me pick out easy classes for the next semester so I could raise my GPA and recuperate at the same time.

Now look at me! I'm hoping I haven't gotten my days mixed up as I rush to what I hope are the correct classes. I'm just like everyone else! Writing a huge thesis shouldn't feel this wonderful. As much fun as this is, I still can't wait until it's over.

Graduation...

Finally it's graduation day. I can't stop grinning! I continue to smile even when my face starts to hurt. Even when the dumb graduation song makes me cry. I look great. I *feel* great! I'm on my way. To where I have no idea.

We stand in line, waiting. Packed in a heated dome filled to capacity, the onlookers stare at the graduates. Some bored, some envious, most proud—*all* tired. The speaker drones on and on about moving ahead, what life is all about, yada yada yada. Finally he starts calling the names of the graduates. I can feel the graduates around me—as well as myself—take a deep breath and stand up straight. I'm sure we all have butterflies in our stomachs. We inch forward every few seconds. Our feet ache. I feel my stomach growl and turn. I still can't wipe the grin off my face. I reach the front. The person in front of me has barely reached the stage when my name is called. *They sure do like to rush!* I speed walk across the stage, trying not to break into a run. The woman standing next to the table piled high with degrees hands me mine and smiles. I smile into the crowd, wondering where Mom, Ram and Jeff are sitting. I skip down the steps. I'm finished! I'm a graduate! I'm not a college student anymore! I'm a grownup! For the first time, I realize that I'm done. That it's all over. I'm overcome with a feeling of accomplishment. Or is it relief? I'm guessing it's partly relief that it's finally over mixed in with the adrenaline rush I now have, but who cares! I'm done! These thoughts run through my head as I meet up with Angela and run backstage. Soon everyone's name has been called. The speaker tries to give his closing speech. The audience is restless. Soon they are pushing their way out the door. They're still tightly packed together, but in the coolness of the afternoon breeze, no one cares. *Wow! It was hotter in there than I thought!* Angela and I run outside and look around for Mom.

Flash! Flash! Flash! I see cameras everywhere. Can a picture really capture what I'm feeling right now? A smile can only say so much.

We pose, hug, laugh and celebrate. A good friend of the family takes pictures of Angela and me, and then each of us individually. Angela, Ram, his friend Casey, Mom's friend David, Jeff and I move in circles around each other, trying to figure out how to arrange ourselves for the group picture. Mom takes control. Soon all of us direct cheesy grins to a happy stranger who has agreed to play photographer. I take a picture of Ram and Casey acting silly. I take a few more pictures of the people around me. I want to remember this day.

I wonder what will happen after I get a job and move away. All my friends will move on, too. I haven't had a seizure in two years, so I can get my license now. Maybe even buy a car. Jeff doesn't graduate until next year. I can't imagine marrying him and having kids. Not right now, anyway. Will we wind up separating after I move away? My stomach begins to turn, so I push these thoughts aside and give Jeff another hug. We all head over to Mom's friend David's house for the celebration party. The huge cake reads, *Congratulations Amanda and Angelica.* Angela doesn't seem to mind. The cake tastes good.

Some kids grow up knowing only the world in which they were born. They feel safe, protected and invincible. All the tough times I faced growing up seemed so unfair. All the moving, the seizures, not being able to afford a high school yearbook my junior year.... Perhaps it was all a test. Perhaps I'm actually the lucky one. I've caught a glimpse of the world beyond the white picket fence. I have the strength to endure the next stage of life—whatever that may be.

INFORMATION ON EPILEPSY

What is Epilepsy?

Epilepsy is defined as a seizure disorder; the tendency to have recurrent seizures.

The brain is like a computer that consists of a large network of nerve cells called neurons. Electrical messages are fired between these cells, controlling our thoughts, actions and emotions. A seizure occurs when a sudden burst of excess electrical activity temporarily disrupts the normal messages passing between brain cells so that the messages become scrambled.

There are two different kinds of seizures—generalized and partial. The kind of seizure that occurs will depend on where the change in brain activity begins and how widely and rapidly it spreads out.

Generalized seizures involve the whole brain. Several types of generalized seizures include tonic-clonic (grandmal), absence (petitemal), and myoclonic. During a grandmal seizure, the muscles in the body tense and relax over and over (called convulsions). The eyes roll back, breathing may become shallow, the skin bluish, and a loss of bladder control when the muscles relax. Another generalized seizure which is common in children with epilepsy is the absence—

or petitemal—seizure. This seizure consists of a blank stare and rapid blinking. Children may drop what they are holding, but quickly return to normal when the seizure stops. Petitemals are often overlooked by others and dismissed as klutziness or daydreaming.

Partial seizures start in just one part of the brain. The electrical discharge may stay in one spot or may spread to the rest of the brain.

Spotting a Seizure—the Symptoms

Because there are many different kinds of seizures and every person is different, seizures affect each of us in a different way. Amounts of stress or other factors that bring on a seizure also vary with each person.

Although some people with epilepsy have seizures that come out of the blue, when controlled by medication, the seizures may have been triggered by stress and other factors.

Possible triggers:

Alcohol—A little bit of alcohol is okay, but alcohol in excess can slow down the effectiveness of anti-epileptic medications.

Stress—Some of us experience seizures during times of stress. Because stress is a part of everyday life, we who have epilepsy need to find ways of keeping it at a minimum.

Patterns of light—Some people with epilepsy who are photosensitive have trouble with flickering light. Some extreme cases include watching TV, working on the computer and playing video games. Other less extreme cases include only strobe lights, fluorescent lights and flashing lights from police cars.

Late nights and lack of sleep—Too many late nights or going without sleep can trigger seizures. One late night should not matter much, but two or more can cause a problem. It is best to try and keep regular hours.

Illness—Fevers and other illnesses that slow down our body's ability to function properly can trigger a seizure. This is more common in young children than adults, although it still reduces a person's seizure threshold, making seizures more likely.

Hormones—Most women with epilepsy experience seizures right before or during the first few days of their menstrual cycle.

Food—Skipping meals and eating an unbalanced diet may trigger seizures.

Living With Epilepsy

Make sure your child is diagnosed by a neurologist who specializes in epilepsy. However, do not rely solely on your doctor for all the information you need on epilepsy. It is important for you to do as much research as you can yourself. Learn about epilepsy and similar neurological disorders. Remember, you know your child better than anyone, so research medications yourself and see which ones you feel most comfortable with.

Thankfully, many teachers today are now required to take a class on special education. Chances are, your child's teachers may already know about epilepsy since it is a common disorder. Inform them of your child's condition anyway, so they are prepared to help your child if he has a seizure during class. If the teachers are not accommodating and you feel your child is being treated unfairly, do not be afraid to stand up for your child. Study the federal and state laws that protect children with disabilities from discrimination on the basis of disability. Do not allow yourself to be bullied. Be an advocate for your child!

At the moment, there is no cure for epilepsy. There are, however, many kinds of medications to help control the seizures so your child can live a relatively normal life. Being diagnosed with epilepsy can lower a one's self-esteem, and even more so with children. This can cause a child to do poorly in school and keep him from interacting with other children. There are many things a parent can do to avoid this.

Be open about epilepsy. Discuss with your child and his siblings the facts about epilepsy so they are not scared or feel guilty about what is happening to him.

Do not discuss your child's seizures or the financial burden of medical care in front of him.

Encourage your child in his skills and hobbies. Praise his successes.

Encourage your child to make friends.

Do not use epilepsy as an excuse to not discipline your child or avoid family activities.

Do not become overly protective of your child. A child with epilepsy can still participate in activities like swimming if he is closely watched by a responsible adult and the seizures are controlled by medication.

Do not feel guilty about taking some time out for yourself. Everyone needs a break from their kids, whether they have disabilities or not.

There are several ways that you can change your child's lifestyle to help reduce the risk of seizures.

Keep stress to a minimum

Plan days to allow time for work, rest and play

Pace your child; make sure he takes breaks

Create regular meals and a healthy diet

Have your child exercise regularly and participate in the sports he likes

Stick to a regular bedtime schedule to avoid getting overly tired

Plan to bring a sufficient amount of medication when traveling away from home

Have a plan for dealing with seizures

Keep a sense of perspective—no one's life can be entirely risk-free. You need to be sensible about what your child can do yet be careful not to let epilepsy rule your child's existence.

Driving—In the U.S., each state has their own rules regarding driving. In Illinois, a person who hasn't had a seizure for 6 months is allowed to get a driver's license, with written consent from their doctor. These regulations were made because unless the seizures are fully controlled by medication, a person with epilepsy can have a seizure while driving which could be fatal.

Welfare—Those with epilepsy who have trouble controlling their seizures can qualify for Medicaid and/or Medicare, as well as a disability check through Social Security.

Emergency Response

When you see someone having a seizure the proper response is to move them carefully away from any sharp edges around them, roll them on their side, put something soft underneath their head, take off their glasses if they are wearing any, and keep their hands away from their face. Do not, however, try to restrain them. *Never* put objects in the person's mouth. A person cannot swallow their tongue. That is a myth. Most likely they will simply bite the edges of their tongue.

If the seizure lasts for more than five minutes or is followed by more seizures, call the paramedics.

What happens to most people after a seizure is headache and disorientation. The best way to help them recover is to have them take a nap and let the brain relax.